MONSTERS & URBAN MYTHS AND LEGENDARY CREATURES

By Lisa Regan and Chris McNab

Gareth Stevens Publishing

Please visit our Web site, www.garethstevens.com. For a free color catalog of all our high-quality books, call toll free 1-800-542-2595 or fax 1-877-542-2596.

Library of Congress Cataloging-in-Publication Data

Regan, Lisa.
Urban myths and legendary creatures / Lisa Regan and Chris McNab.
p. cm.
 ISBN 978-1-4339-5009-4 (library binding)
 ISBN 978-1-4339-5010-0 (pbk.)
 ISBN 978-1-4339-5011-7 (6-pack)
1. Animals, Mythical. 2. Legends. I. McNab, Chris. II. Title.
GR825.R44 2011
398.24'54–dc22
2010039134

Published in 2011 by
Gareth Stevens Publishing
111 East 14th Street, Suite 349
New York, NY 10003

Copyright © 2011 Amber Books Ltd, London

Illustrations copyright © Amber Books and IMP AB

All rights reserved. No part of this book may be reproduced in any form without permission in writing from the publisher, except by a reviewer.

Printed in the United States of America

CPSIA compliance information: Batch #CW11GS: For further information contact Gareth Stevens, New York, New York at 1-800-542-2595.

Table of Contents

The Beast of Bray Road 4
Bigfoot 6
Bunyip 8
Goatman 10
Hopkinsville Goblin 12
Jersey Devil 14
Kongamoto 16
Loch Ness Monster 18
Mngwa 20
Mokele-Mbembe 22
Morgawr 24
Nandi Bear 26
Ogopogo 28
Reptoid Alien 30
Skunk Ape 32
Spring Heeled Jack 34
Thetis Lake Monster 36
Tokoloshe 38
Yara-ma-yha-who 40
Yeti 42
Guide to Urban Myths and Legendary Creatures 44
Glossary 46
For More Information 47
Index 48

URBAN MYTHS AND LEGENDARY CREATURES

The Beast of Bray Road

BODY
The beast is described as having a large, heavy body and powerful chest, like that of a person who works out at the gym.

HEAD
Like a wild animal, the beast has a snout, pointed ears, and large fangs. Its eyes glow yellow, like an animal caught in the headlights.

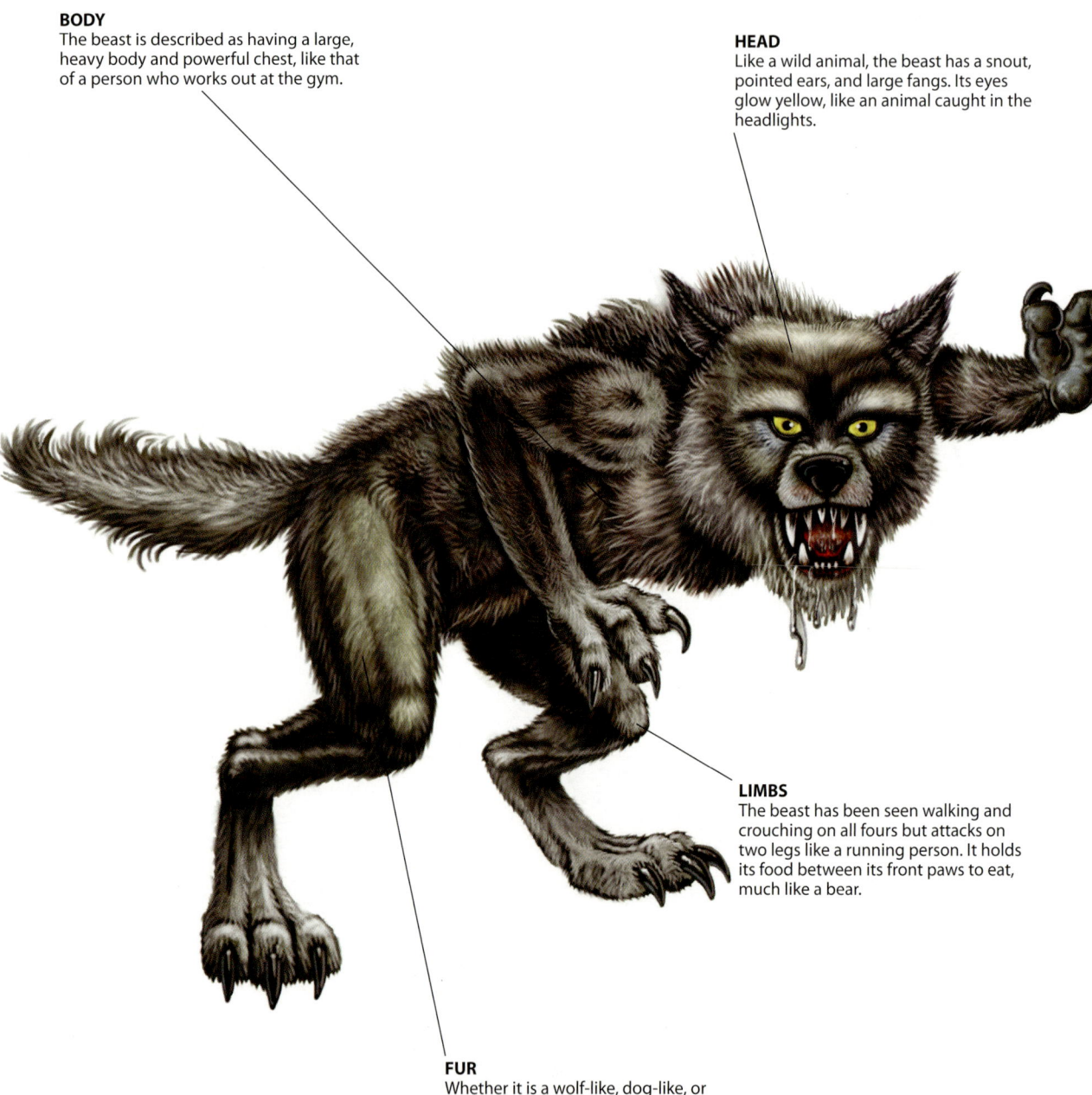

LIMBS
The beast has been seen walking and crouching on all fours but attacks on two legs like a running person. It holds its food between its front paws to eat, much like a bear.

FUR
Whether it is a wolf-like, dog-like, or bear-like creature, it is always said to have gray-brown hair all over its body.

THE BEAST OF BRAY ROAD

Is the Beast of Bray Road an actual werewolf? It depends on what, and who, you believe. In the 1980s and 1990s, there were many sightings of this creature, skulking in the undergrowth and looking for meat to eat. Most people described it as a large, strong, heavy, and hairy creature. They didn't always agree on what kind of animal it most resembled. One thing is for sure, though—the beast doesn't eat people. Moviemakers have turned the beast into a more sinister creature that terrorizes humans and eats them, but in real life it seems that it would rather run away than attack a human.

ACTUAL SIZE

⚠ One man who saw the Beast was working at night, collecting roadkill to keep the highways clear. He was sitting at the roadside in his truck, filling out paperwork, when the truck began to shake. In his mirror, he could see a large, furry beast. It was standing on two legs and helping itself to a deer from the back of the truck. The Beast had found a ready meal for supper! The man quickly drove off, frightened, and when he returned only five minutes later, both creature and deer had disappeared.

WHERE IN THE WORLD?

Bray Road is a two-mile (3.2-km) stretch of road through Wisconsin farmland, but the Beast has been seen in many areas in the southeast of the state.

DID YOU KNOW?

- **Cryptozoologists (scientists in search of new creatures and proof that they exist) think that the Beast might be some kind of Bigfoot.**

- **The Beast is reported as being 7 feet (2.1 m) tall and weighing maybe 200 pounds (91 kg).**

- **A journalist named Linda Godfrey has spent many years researching sightings of the creature. She says that a large number of the sightings are reported near sacred Native American sites such as burial grounds.**

- **Strange happenings in the area—mutilated animal bodies and unusual lights in the night sky—have led some people to believe in an occult or supernatural link to the creature. They think it could certainly be a shape-shifter like a werewolf.**

URBAN MYTHS AND LEGENDARY CREATURES

Bigfoot

SIZE
Bigfoot measures more than 3 feet 3 inches (1 m) wide and has a stooping posture and broad, sloping shoulders. Its weight is estimated at 400 to 440 pounds (181 to 200 kg).

ARMS
The arms are long in proportion to the body, hanging down to the knees or even below.

FACE
Bigfoot has a heavy brow ridge and wide, ape-like nostrils. Its eyes may shine green or yellow.

HAIR
One of Bigfoot's most distinctive features is a thick covering of hair. Usually, this coat is shaggy and brown, but some people have described it as rust-colored, black, or even glossy.

BIGFOOT

This terrifying, ape-like creature is said to roam in remote mountain forests, but it has eluded researchers and baffled skeptics for more than 150 years. Standing well over 6 feet 6 inches (2 m) high, with arms down to its knees, Bigfoot can easily carry away dogs and livestock. More than 1,600 instances of Bigfoot sightings or trails have been recorded in the United States and Canada since the early 19th century.

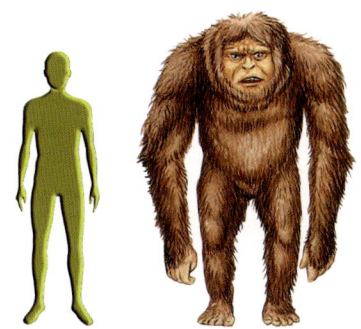

ACTUAL SIZE

▶ GIGANTOPITHECUS
This giant ape was the largest primate ever to live on Earth. Fossils of two species have been found in India and China, dating from between one and nine million years ago. Scientists think the ape lived in open country, but they don't know if it walked upright.

▶ YETI
Although there have been few actual sightings of the Himalayan abominable snowman, or yeti, many people have come across its distinctive tracks. Some who have seen the yeti describe a creature with pale or white hair, while others report a darker coat and a pointed head.

▶ ALMA
This "wild man" of Central Asia is reputedly smaller than Bigfoot and less ape-like in build. In the late 1950s, based on his research into reported sightings, Soviet scientist Boris Porshnev suggested that these "wild men" were remnant populations of Neanderthals.

WHERE IN THE WORLD?

More than 400 reports of Bigfoot sightings come from California, Oregon, and Washington, and from the Canadian province of British Columbia. Other sightings have been reported from almost every part of Canada and the United States.

DID YOU KNOW?

• Many people who have shot at Bigfoot from point-blank range report that the creature seems invulnerable to gunfire.

• In 1995, a sample of alleged Bigfoot hair was sent for DNA analysis at Ohio State University. After years of testing, the results are still inconclusive.

• Hunters claim their dogs shy away from Bigfoot, whimpering.

URBAN MYTHS AND LEGENDARY CREATURES

Bunyip

BODY
Although water bound, some sightings of the Bunyip report it to be dark and hairy, at least the size of a calf. Others say it is covered in scales.

NOISE
The bellowing call of the Bunyip can be heard for miles around, like a loud booming coming from the water.

FACE
In some descriptions, the Bunyip has only a single eye in its fearsome head. In others, it has two eyes that blaze like fire from its face.

CLAWS
Bunyip has giant clawed hands, which help it to climb out of its watery home and even allow it to drag itself up trees.

BUNYIP

Native Australians have many tales of a water monster called Bunyip. It lives in swamps, billabongs, and other still inland waters, and many times keeps to itself if it is left alone. However, it should not be disturbed, especially if it has a Bunyip cub to protect. It has the power to swell the waters to cover even the highest points on land, and to wash over the tops of trees. It can turn humans into black swans, or change women into beautiful water spirits who can tempt men to their death with their songs of love.

▲ A man from the Frog tribe was hunting in the lagoon while his son waited on the bank. Suddenly a Bunyip rose from the waters and dragged off the boy in his long arms. Every day, the man returned and laid frogs as bait to catch the Bunyip. Then one night the Bunyip appeared, and the man saw his son under its spell. He reached out to his son, but he became trapped, too. At last, a great storm blew up and broke the spell, and since then the tribe have never hurt the frogs that helped trap Bunyip.

ACTUAL SIZE

WHERE IN THE WORLD?

Many tales of Bunyip are told across all of Australia. In Tasmania, it is also called Good Hope and Universal Eye.

DID YOU KNOW?

• If a Bunyip cub is taken by humans, the mother will make all the waters rise and pour into the houses until she gets her child back. Nowhere is safe. The waters can climb hills and cover trees.

• A Bunyip's spell spreads around it in a circle, and entrances anyone who gets too close.

• "Sightings" of the Bunyip are still reported to this day. Some describe it as a large dog-like creature, while others say it has a very long neck. Sometimes it has tusks, flippers, or feathers, or looks like a horse.

• Many Bunyip sightings are thought to be people hiding from the law. It is easy to hide in deserted water holes, and anyone coming up for air would be a strange sight, covered in dirt and weeds.

URBAN MYTHS AND LEGENDARY CREATURES

Goatman

HEAD
Part goat, part human, this face is one to haunt your nightmares. It has a goat's horns, eyes, and snout set in a strangely human face.

BODY
The creature has the legs and hooves of a goat, but its top half is the body of a man, although it is covered in tufts of black hair.

AXE
Goatman wields a giant, sharpened ax, which it uses to break through car windshields.

LEGS
Like a true goat, Goatman has incredibly strong, springy legs that allow it to leap onto cars and run away very quickly.

GOATMAN

From the 1960s or 1970s, tales of Goatman have driven fear into the hearts of couples in America. This Maryland monster is driven with jealousy and hatred for those who have what he doesn't—good looks, a person to love them, and a normal life. For it is thought that Goatman is the result of a sophisticated science experiment that went horribly wrong. The scientist in charge of animal research was caught in a short circuit and found himself transformed into a billy goat–human mutation. He grabbed an ax as a weapon and ran, and has been terrorizing people ever since.

⚠ It's not uncommon for a boyfriend to take his girlfriend out for a drive, so they can share some time alone together. They must beware, though, because isolated lanes are the Goatman's favorite haunt. First, his goat-shaped shadow appears on the hood of the car. Then his twisted billy-goat face looms at the window, his eyes filled with jealousy and rage. He hacks through the windshield as the couple clings to each other, trapped, and then he takes one or both of them as his prize (and supper).

ACTUAL SIZE

WHERE IN THE WORLD?

Couples in and around Prince George's County in Maryland live in fear of being followed by Goatman.

DID YOU KNOW?

• Goatman attacks because of bitterness and hatred but also for food. If he cannot find humans, he will take family pets and livestock. At worst, he is like any other goat and will eat whatever is available: plants, berries, eggs, and even garbage.

• Goat-based figures are often linked with Satan, developed from the pagan god of nature, Pan, who was part goat.

• One of the Goatman's favorite places is Crybaby Bridge in Prince George's County, where it is said that the crying of a ghost—a baby that was drowned under the bridge—can be heard at night.

• There is also a Goatman in Texas, who was seen in 1972, and around the United States from Oregon to Oklahoma.

URBAN MYTHS AND LEGENDARY CREATURES

Hopkinsville Goblin

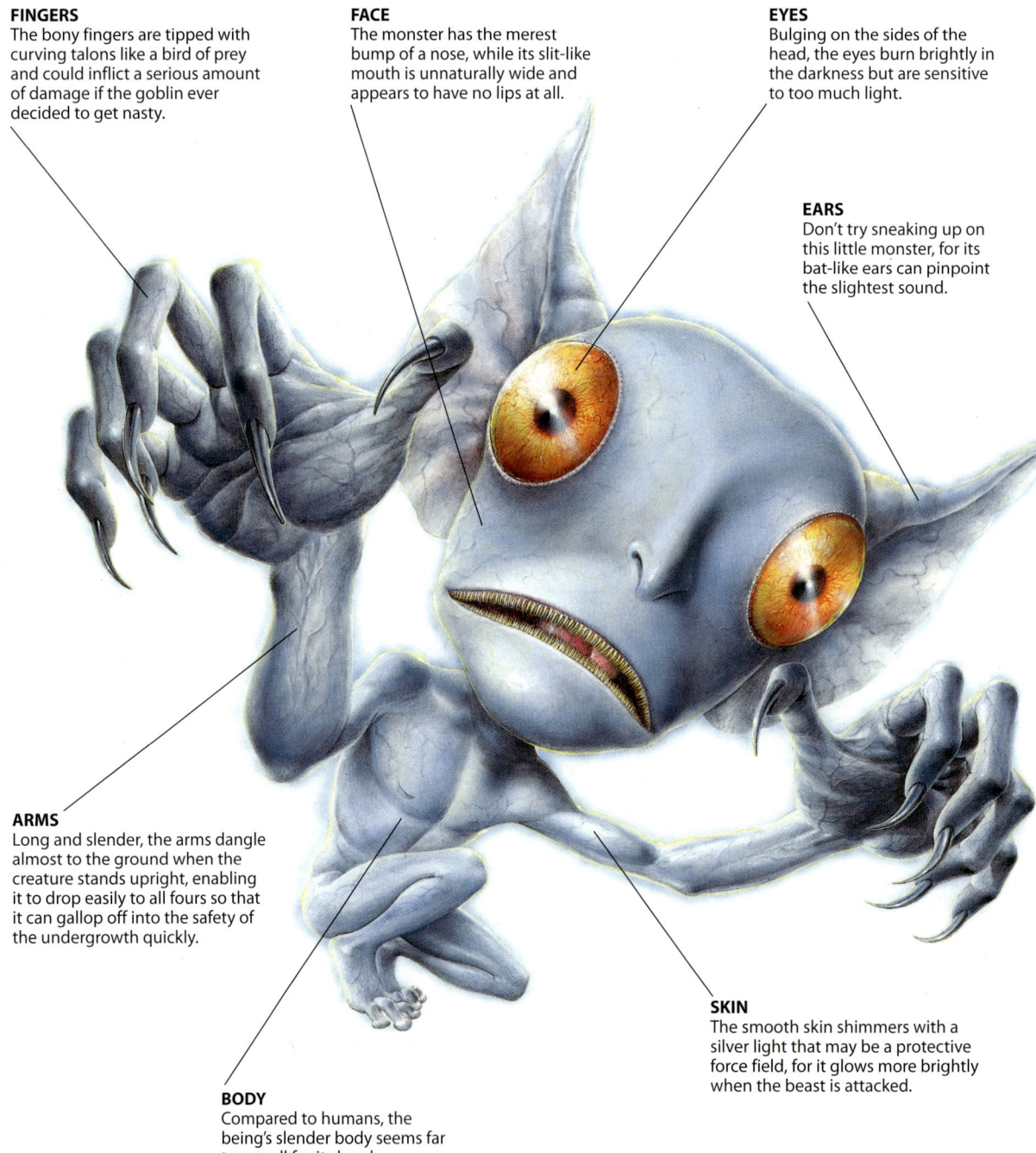

FINGERS
The bony fingers are tipped with curving talons like a bird of prey and could inflict a serious amount of damage if the goblin ever decided to get nasty.

FACE
The monster has the merest bump of a nose, while its slit-like mouth is unnaturally wide and appears to have no lips at all.

EYES
Bulging on the sides of the head, the eyes burn brightly in the darkness but are sensitive to too much light.

EARS
Don't try sneaking up on this little monster, for its bat-like ears can pinpoint the slightest sound.

ARMS
Long and slender, the arms dangle almost to the ground when the creature stands upright, enabling it to drop easily to all fours so that it can gallop off into the safety of the undergrowth quickly.

SKIN
The smooth skin shimmers with a silver light that may be a protective force field, for it glows more brightly when the beast is attacked.

BODY
Compared to humans, the being's slender body seems far too small for its head.

HOPKINSVILLE GOBLIN

Alien or supernatural creature? No one knows the origin of the Hopkinsville Goblin, but Elmer Sutton saw one clearly enough to shoot it in a tree on his Kentucky farm. Local Cherokee Indians also had traditions of visiting nighttime creatures that perfectly matched Sutton's description of what he saw. The case remains a mystery, but tales of goblins have featured in folklore since the earliest times. They are known as mischievous creatures, hiding out in underground grottoes, hollow tree trunks, or hidden areas around the house, emerging after dark to scare local humans. A few goblins are malevolent in nature and have been known to get downright nasty.

⚠ Creeping outside to investigate sounds, Elmer Sutton spotted a goblin sitting in a tree, and taking aim with his shotgun, he blasted it from its perch. But instead of tumbling to the ground, the eerie creature recovered in midair and floated toward its terrified attacker before scampering off into a bush.

ACTUAL SIZE

WHERE IN THE WORLD?

The only documented sighting of the Hopkinsville Goblins occurred at the Suttons' farm near Kelly (sometimes known as Kelly Station), which is situated just north of the town of Hopkinsville, Kentucky.

DID YOU KNOW?

• Investigators combed the area around the farm for clues, but the only signs of the encounter were stray bullet holes, although one policeman did see a faint luminous patch on the grass where one of the goblins fell.

• Local Cherokee people tell of wide-eyed beings that shunned the light and had to be chased off when one of their tribes moved to a new hunting ground. So it seems that odd humanoids have appeared before.

URBAN MYTHS AND LEGENDARY CREATURES

Jersey Devil

HORNS
Two goat-like horns top the creature's head, enhancing its devilish appearance.

HEAD
The creature's head is similar to that of a donkey, but with a dog's nose and teeth. Its gums are rotten and its breath so foul that it curdles milk, blights crops, and poisons rivers and lakes, killing fish.

WINGS
The leathery wings resemble those of a bat, and some say their span is surprisingly small, stretching to just 26 inches (65 cm) when fully unfurled.

BODY
The body is that of a dog or horse. Though it's muscular, it's lithe in form for slipping down narrow chimneys, and emits a yellowish hue as the beast flies at night.

TAIL
Some say the tail is tipped with a tuft, others that it ends with a three-pointed spike like that of the devil.

FORELEGS
Each leg ends in a cloven hoof, but the forelegs are relatively short and stubby, and seldom used.

HIND LEGS
The Jersey Devil often walks upright on its two hind legs, which some witnesses describe as being long and spindly like those of a crane.

JERSEY DEVIL

The bleak marshes of New Jersey have never welcomed people, and locals tell of strange sightings and chilling cries in the dark. According to many, something evil is out there. With bat-like wings and the head of a deformed horse, this inexplicable beast has been terrifying locals for more than 200 years. The devil emerges in the dead of night to haunt the countryside, killing wild and domestic animals and abducting small children. In January 1909, in a single week, more than 1,000 people said they came face-to-face with the Jersey Devil, which appeared to home owners, policemen, and local officials. The accounts were all very similar, and local and national newspapers were forced to take the story seriously.

 Driven mad by hunger, the Jersey Devil leaves its dismal swampy home and flies to a nearby town, a glowing shadow in the night sky. After cruising over the rooftops, it spots a suitable chimney and dives swiftly down the soot-laden stack. The devil is unscathed by the fierce fire burning in the grate and bursts through the flames, scattering logs into the kitchen beyond. Screaming in terror at the nightmare vision, a maid watches in horror as the devil makes for the pantry. She can only pray that the child upstairs remains silent—for a single cry might tempt the ravenous beast to sample fresher food…

WHERE IN THE WORLD?

Many sightings of the Jersey Devil occur in the Pine Barrens of New Jersey: a lonely area of swamps and cedar forests covering 1,698 sq miles (4,400 sq km). But other reports come from all around the state and occasionally from across the border.

ACTUAL SIZE

DID YOU KNOW?

• In 1909, the Philadelphia Zoo offered a $10,000 reward for the capture of the devil. This has prompted several hoaxes, including a painted kangaroo with a set of false wings. The reward remains to be claimed to this day.

• When the rotting corpse of a strange, devilish creature was found in the Pine Barrens in 1957, many people took this as evidence that the Jersey Devil was dead. But since then there have been several sightings.

URBAN MYTHS AND LEGENDARY CREATURES

Kongamoto

WINGS
The creature has wings more like a bat than a bird, as they appear leathery and made of skin, without feathers.

HEAD
Kongamoto has a bird-like head that is dominated by the beak and a strange crest that sticks up from the top of the forehead, above the eyes.

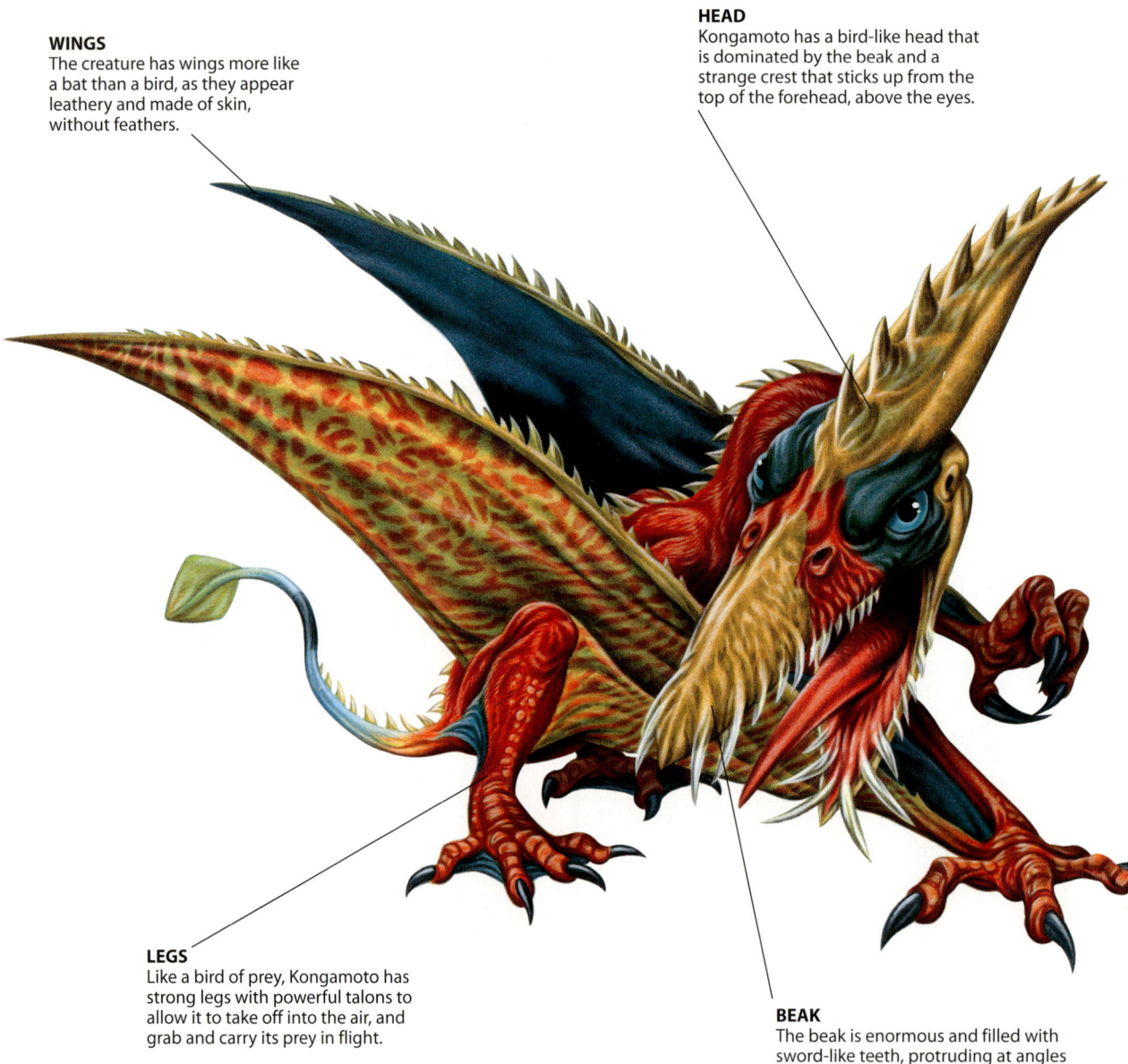

LEGS
Like a bird of prey, Kongamoto has strong legs with powerful talons to allow it to take off into the air, and grab and carry its prey in flight.

BEAK
The beak is enormous and filled with sword-like teeth, protruding at angles from the inside and outside of the bill.

KONGAMOTO

This creature is called Kongamoto by the local people of southern Africa. The name means "overwhelmer of boats," for it is said to capsize canoes. It is described as a flying reptile, as it has no feathers and no fur but is scaly like a lizard. It can cause death to anyone who looks at it, and has a wicked appetite for human and animal flesh. Only a few people live to escape its clutches and make it out of the forests and swamps where it lives and hunts. Some people believe it is a pterosaur, the flying reptile that lived with the dinosaurs 65 million years ago.

▲ Very few people are willing to enter the "Swamp of Demons" where Kongamoto is said to live. Some, however, stumble across its home by accident. One young man traveling through the jungle heard the deathly shrieking of a creature like none he had heard before. With no time to turn and run, he found himself under attack from the screeching beast. Swooping like an eagle, the Kongamoto tore into his flesh, but then strangely flew into the undergrowth. The poor man was able to drag himself back to his people and tell his unusual tale.

ACTUAL SIZE

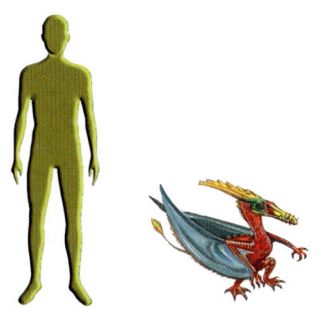

WHERE IN THE WORLD?

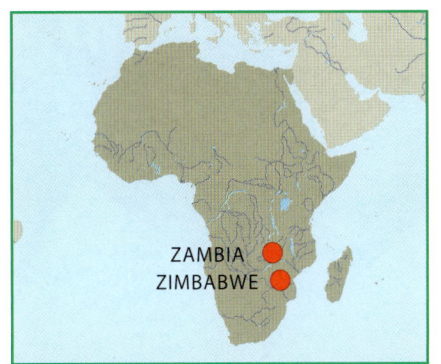

Many people in southern Africa are frightened of Kongamoto. Most sightings happen in Zambia and Zimbabwe.

DID YOU KNOW?

• The Kongamoto is said to eat rotting human flesh, and will dig up bodies if they are not buried deeply enough.

• Tales are also told in Namibia and Cameroon of a creature very similar to the Kongamoto. The Cameroon natives call theirs Olitau.

• A traveler called Frank H. Melland spent time working in Zambia and heard many tales of Kongamoto from the villagers near the Jiundu swamps. They described the beast that terrorized the area, and when he showed them pictures of a pterodactyl, they instantly said that it was how the monster looked.

• The Kaonde tribe of northwestern Zambia believes that before you cross a river, you must protect yourself against Kongamoto with a special paste called "mulendi," or with a charm called "muchi wa Kongamoto."

URBAN MYTHS AND LEGENDARY CREATURES

Loch Ness Monster

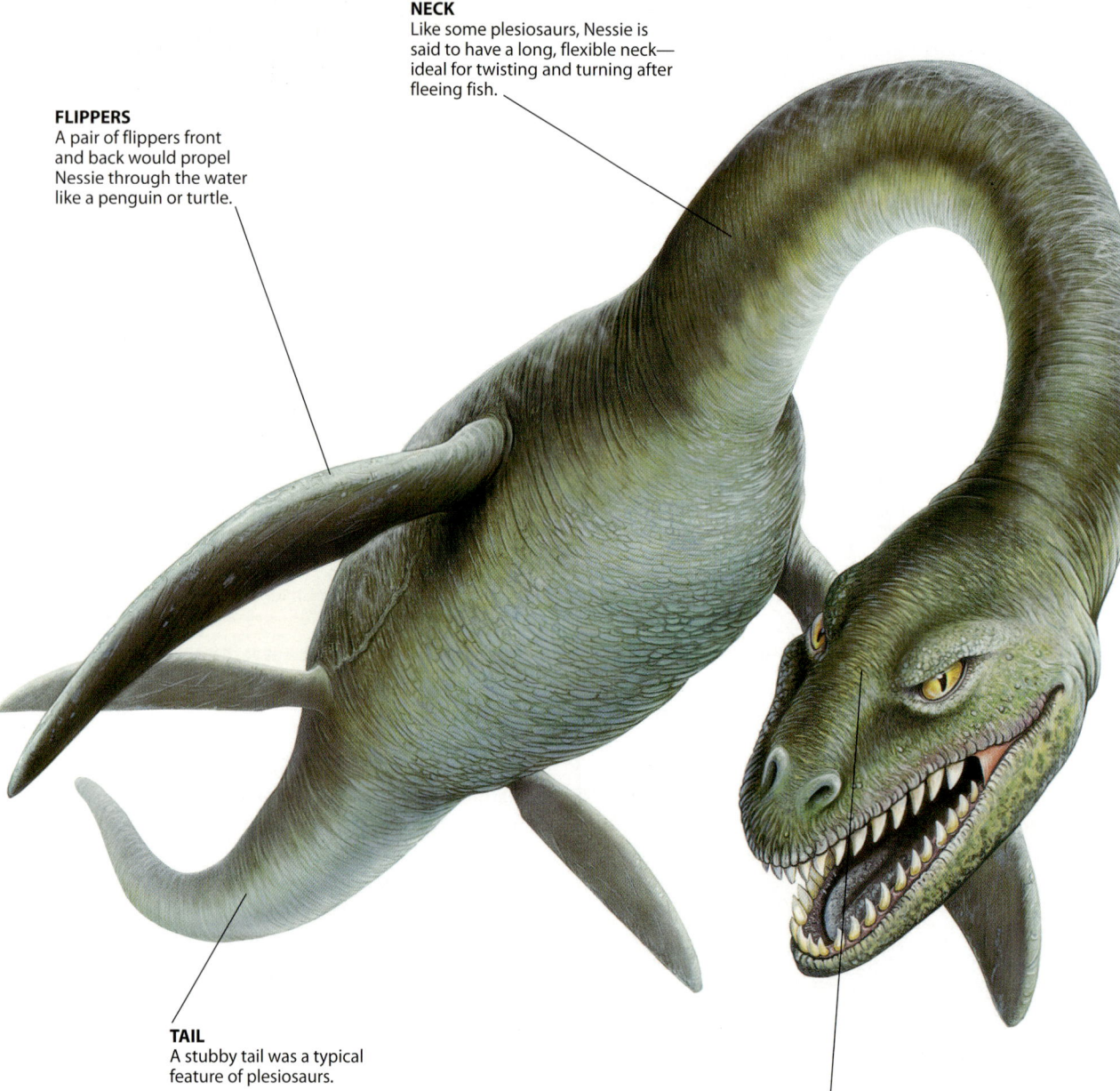

NECK
Like some plesiosaurs, Nessie is said to have a long, flexible neck—ideal for twisting and turning after fleeing fish.

FLIPPERS
A pair of flippers front and back would propel Nessie through the water like a penguin or turtle.

TAIL
A stubby tail was a typical feature of plesiosaurs.

HEAD
Forward-pointing eyes would allow the monster to target fish. Nessie would also need plenty of needle-sharp teeth to seize slippery, wriggling prey.

LOCH NESS MONSTER

Legend has long had it that something strange lurks in the dark depths of Loch Ness—and since the 1930s, thousands of people have claimed to have seen a humpbacked, long-necked beast there. Some people claim that the "Loch Ness Monster" is actually a dinosaur whose species survives to this day in the cold Scottish waters. Other people say that the whole monster story is simply a myth invented by imaginative people.

▶ Some people believe Nessie is a prehistoric whale called Zeuglodon (or Basilosaurus), which is thought to have died out 18 million years ago. They say it lived at sea until after the last Ice Age, then adapted to the freshwater of Loch Ness, where its blubber keeps it warm.

▶ Loch Ness is home to brown trout, Arctic char, pike—and millions of European eels, which can grow to 6 feet 6 inches (2 m) in length. Many people who live near the loch believe the monster is nothing more than a large eel.

ACTUAL SIZE

▶ Enormous fish called sturgeon sometimes swim up the River Ness from the sea and enter Loch Ness in search of food or mates. Reaching several feet in length, with lines of humps on their backs, they might explain many of the sightings of Nessie—especially when they are seen chasing salmon near the surface a long way out from the shore.

WHERE IN THE WORLD?

Loch Ness is part of a chain of lochs, rivers, and canals in the Great Glen, a geological fault that runs right across the Scottish Highlands from the North Sea to the Atlantic Ocean. The River Ness links the loch to the North Sea.

DID YOU KNOW?

• There is not a single recorded sighting of Nessie before 1930.

• A handful of claimed sightings have been on land, including one of the first, on July 22, 1933. A couple reported that a monster crossed the road in front of their car as they drove along the loch.

• Scientists who believe the Loch Ness Monster exists have given it a Latin name: *Nessitera rhombopteryx*.

URBAN MYTHS AND LEGENDARY CREATURES

Mngwa

SIZE
The mngwa is huge—as big as a donkey—but capable of the stealthy prowl and killer spring of a big cat.

COLOR
The victims of the creature have sometimes been found clutching handfuls of gray fur. It is described as striped like a tabby cat.

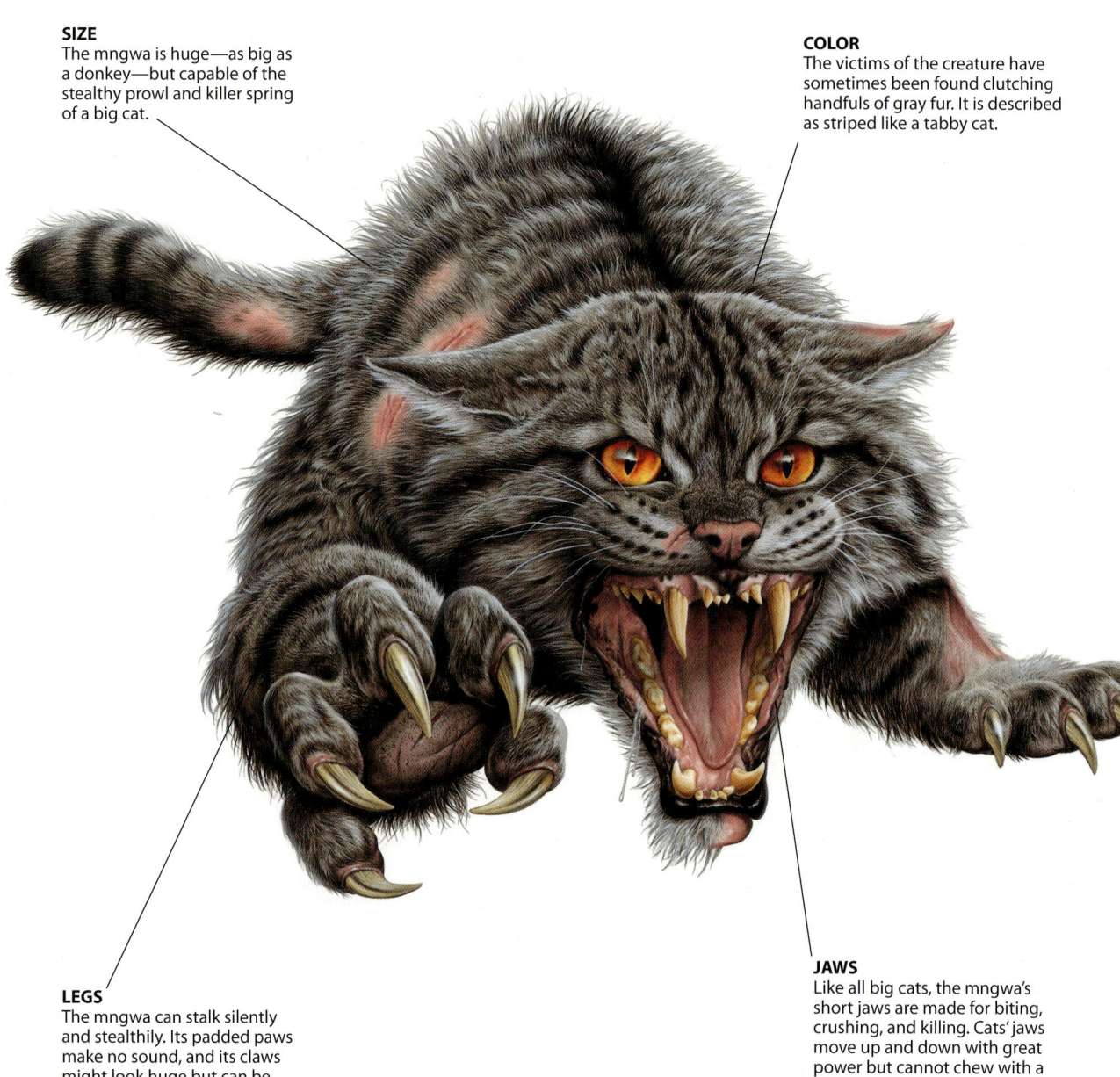

LEGS
The mngwa can stalk silently and stealthily. Its padded paws make no sound, and its claws might look huge but can be pulled back into the toes to stop any noise.

JAWS
Like all big cats, the mngwa's short jaws are made for biting, crushing, and killing. Cats' jaws move up and down with great power but cannot chew with a sideways motion.

MNGWA

This animal, described as the "terror of the coastlands," is as real in the minds of the people of eastern Africa as the lion or the leopard is. They are even more frightened of it, though. Men who will gang up on a lion, armed only with sticks, will not engage in a hunt for the mngwa, even if they have guns. The creature comes out from hiding only to kill its human supper and then disappears without a trace. For centuries, hunting parties have been organized to track down mngwa, but nobody has ever been able to hunt and kill one.

▲ The police are well aware of the belief in the mngwa and are always on the alert for signs of its presence. One young officer was patrolling near a forest when he saw something lying in the rough grass. He drew out his gun and approached with much caution. To his dismay, what he had seen was his partner, bitten, bloodied, and mauled. The man was clutching gray fur in his hand, and the rustle in the grass told him the mngwa was still hungry.

ACTUAL SIZE

WHERE IN THE WORLD?

KENYA
TANZANIA

People in the east African countries of Kenya and Tanzania are as frightened of the mngwa as they are of the lion or leopard.

DID YOU KNOW?

• Its name means the "strange one" in Swahili and it is sometimes also known as the nunda. Its name is pronounced "ming-wa."

• Swahilis sing songs about mngwa hunts by the old rulers, the Sultans, and the stories of the creature are 700 years old.

• The gray hairs of the cat have been sent off for scientific examination. The hairs are not from a lion or leopard but may be from an exceptionally large African golden cat. So why is the creature described as gray in color?

• It has been suggested that some of the 19th-century attacks blamed on the Nandi bear might actually be attacks by the mngwa.

URBAN MYTHS AND LEGENDARY CREATURES

Mokele-Mbembe

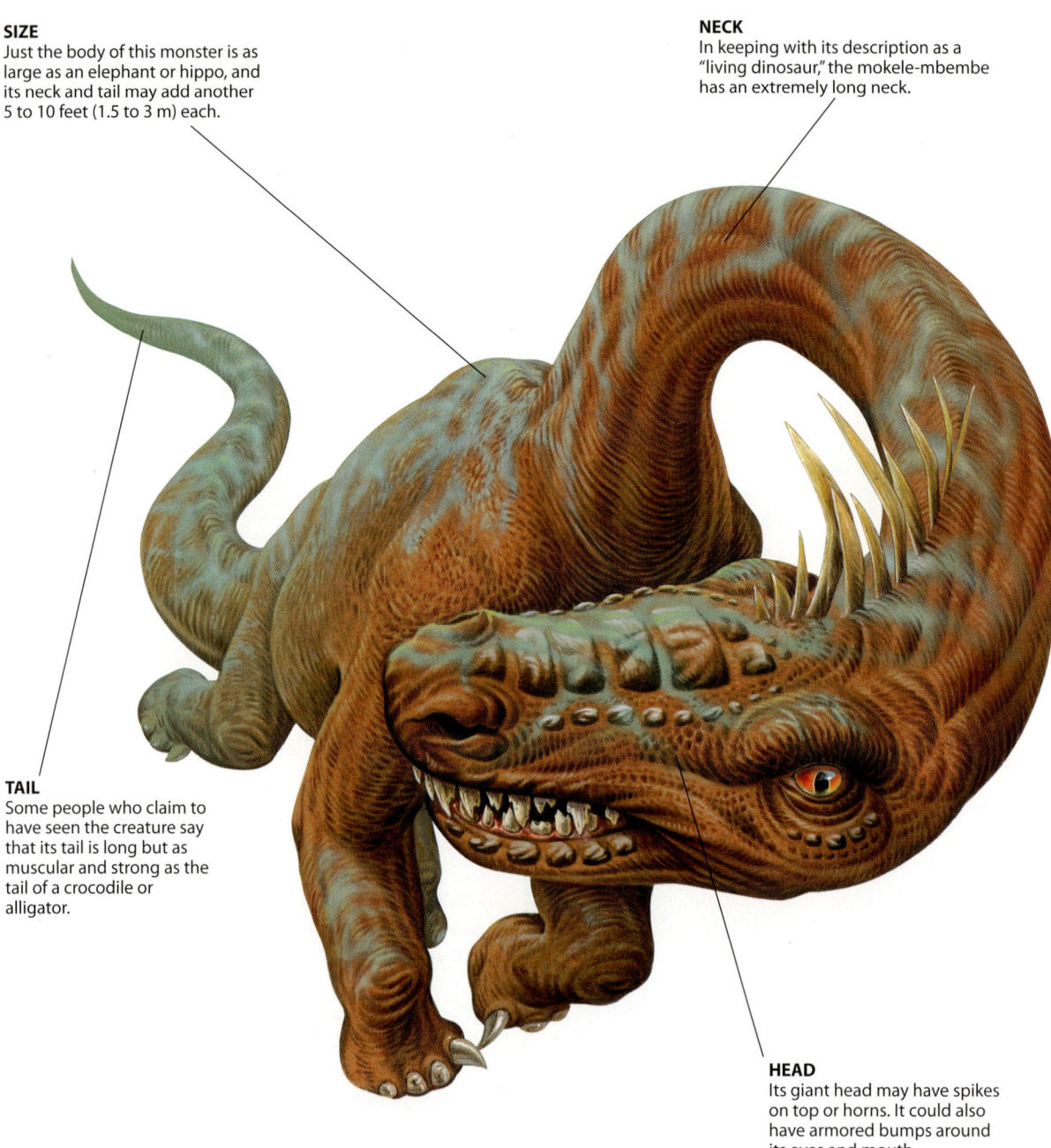

SIZE
Just the body of this monster is as large as an elephant or hippo, and its neck and tail may add another 5 to 10 feet (1.5 to 3 m) each.

NECK
In keeping with its description as a "living dinosaur," the mokele-mbembe has an extremely long neck.

TAIL
Some people who claim to have seen the creature say that its tail is long but as muscular and strong as the tail of a crocodile or alligator.

HEAD
Its giant head may have spikes on top or horns. It could also have armored bumps around its eyes and mouth.

MOKELE-MBEMBE

The earliest people lived on the continent of Africa, and so the world's earliest tales of monsters are located there, too. The mokele-mbembe is a "living dinosaur" that lives around the western coasts of central Africa. It does not eat meat, but it does not like to be disturbed by humans, and becomes very violent if its territory is invaded. It rises up in a rage and overturns boats, casting out the people in them who either drown or are bitten and pummeled by the creature until they have no chance of survival.

In the last 200 years, the tales of mokele-mbembe have changed from myths to reports of real sightings. The Likouala Swamp in the People's Republic of Congo is huge (about the size of Arkansas) and may well be the chosen home of a large, plant-eating creature that hides away from humans and keeps to itself. Natives have found tracks that look like elephant prints but with claws. Strange sounds have been reported coming from the swamplands and undergrowth. Is there really still a dinosaur—or several—alive in Africa today?

ACTUAL SIZE

WHERE IN THE WORLD?

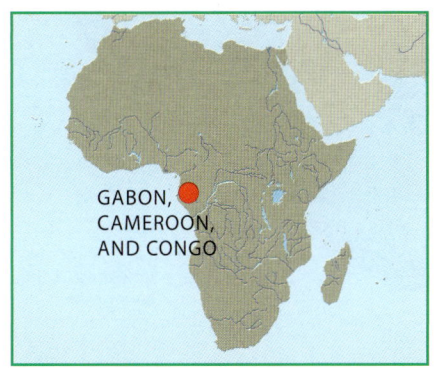

GABON, CAMEROON, AND CONGO

This creature hides in the jungles and around the coasts of the western African countries Gabon, Cameroon, and Congo.

DID YOU KNOW?

• Sightings of the mokele-mbembe have been reported in the 21st century and expeditions to find it were launched in 2000 and 2001. Some researchers truly believe it is out there.

• The creature eats two main types of swamp plants and lives underwater unless it is eating or traveling to a new place to live.

• Its name means "one that stops the flow of rivers." It is regarded as sacred by some tribes, and tales of deaths after killing and eating a mokele-mbembe stop people from hunting it.

• The mokele-mbembe may take the role of the dragon in African stories and is certainly similar to the European folklore of the Loch Ness Monster, another "living dinosaur."

URBAN MYTHS AND LEGENDARY CREATURES

Morgawr

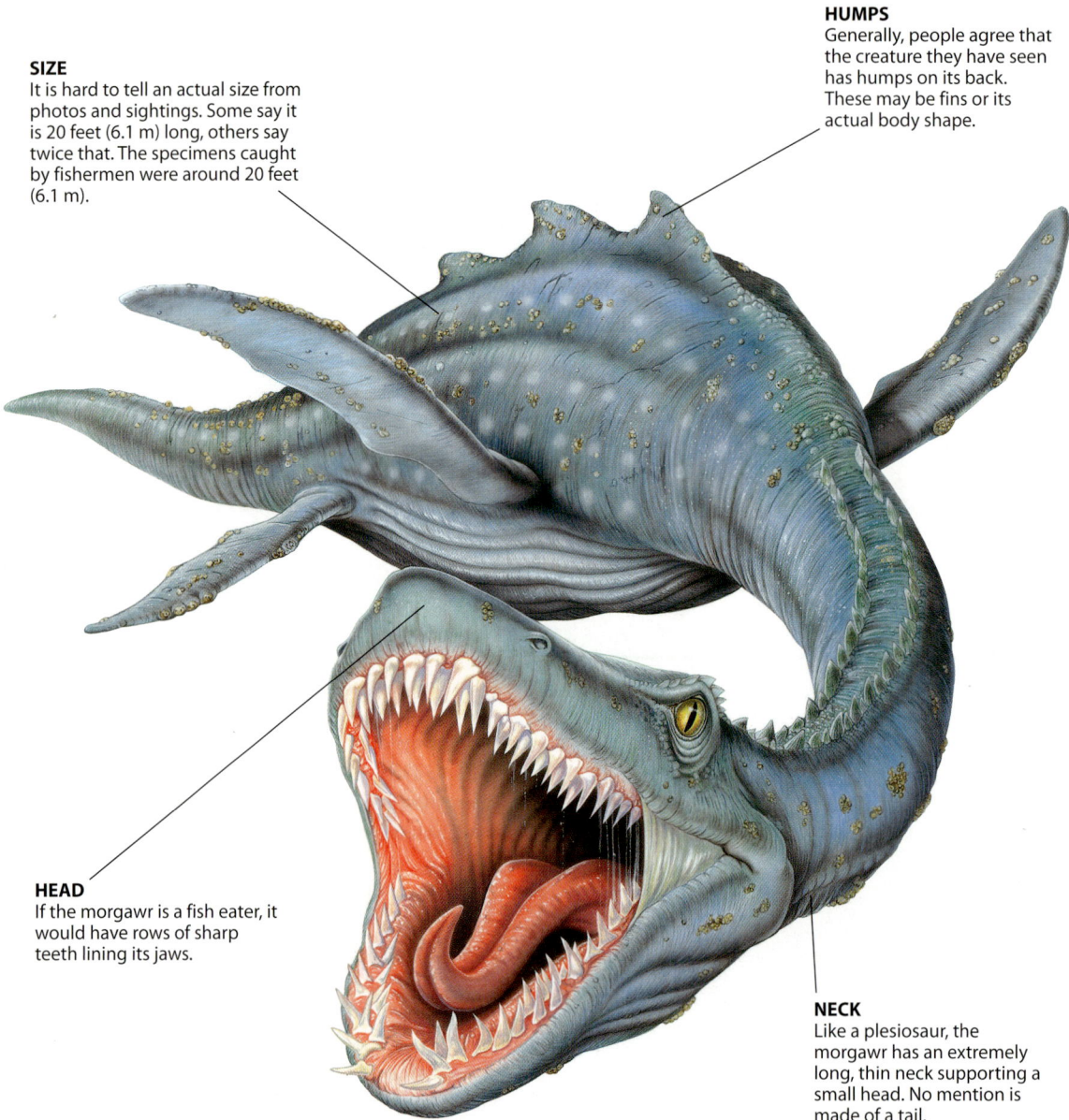

SIZE
It is hard to tell an actual size from photos and sightings. Some say it is 20 feet (6.1 m) long, others say twice that. The specimens caught by fishermen were around 20 feet (6.1 m).

HUMPS
Generally, people agree that the creature they have seen has humps on its back. These may be fins or its actual body shape.

HEAD
If the morgawr is a fish eater, it would have rows of sharp teeth lining its jaws.

NECK
Like a plesiosaur, the morgawr has an extremely long, thin neck supporting a small head. No mention is made of a tail.

MORGAWR

The morgawr is a monster from the southwest coast of England. Its name means "sea giant" in an old Cornish language. The morgawr was first seen in 1876, when two fishermen claimed to have caught a sea serpent. Fifty years later, another was caught. It appears to be similar to the famous Loch Ness Monster from Scotland, with a long neck and large, humped body, except the morgawr lives in salt water, not the freshwater of a loch. It has been suggested that both are plesiosaurs: water-dwelling reptiles from the time of the dinosaurs.

ACTUAL SIZE

After the tales of fishermen catching a sea giant, nothing was seen or heard of the morgawr until the 1970s. Then there were many more sightings, with one woman reporting the creature dived and resurfaced with an eel in its mouth. In 1976, a photograph was taken by "Mary F.," and several local newspapers reported sightings. People flocked to the area to take their own pictures, but the monster appears to be camera shy. A real, valid picture could be worth a fortune, but no one who has camped out to snap the morgawr has had any luck.

WHERE IN THE WORLD?

Most of the sightings are in and around Falmouth in the English county of Cornwall.

DID YOU KNOW?

• Hundreds of people have tried to photograph the monster. A young witch called Pysche tried to entice the morgawr to the surface by swimming in the ocean, and the psychic Tony "Doc" Shields tried to make telepathic contact with the morgawr.

• When journalists tried to track down "Mary F.," she was unable to be found, and the negatives of the prints had been sold to a mystery American. An investigation has suggested that the photos were a hoax by Tony "Doc" Shields.

• Many sightings took place in 1976. Around the same time, in the same area, several UFOs were spotted.

• An employee of the Natural History Museum filmed the monster in 1999, but another expert thinks the footage is only of a sunfish, the heaviest bony fish in the world.

URBAN MYTHS AND LEGENDARY CREATURES

Nandi Bear

SIZE
The Nandi bear is about the size of a large lion, standing around four and a half feet (1.4 m) high from floor to shoulder.

EYE
Some descriptions say the creature has just one eye in the middle of its forehead, although this would seriously restrict its hunting vision.

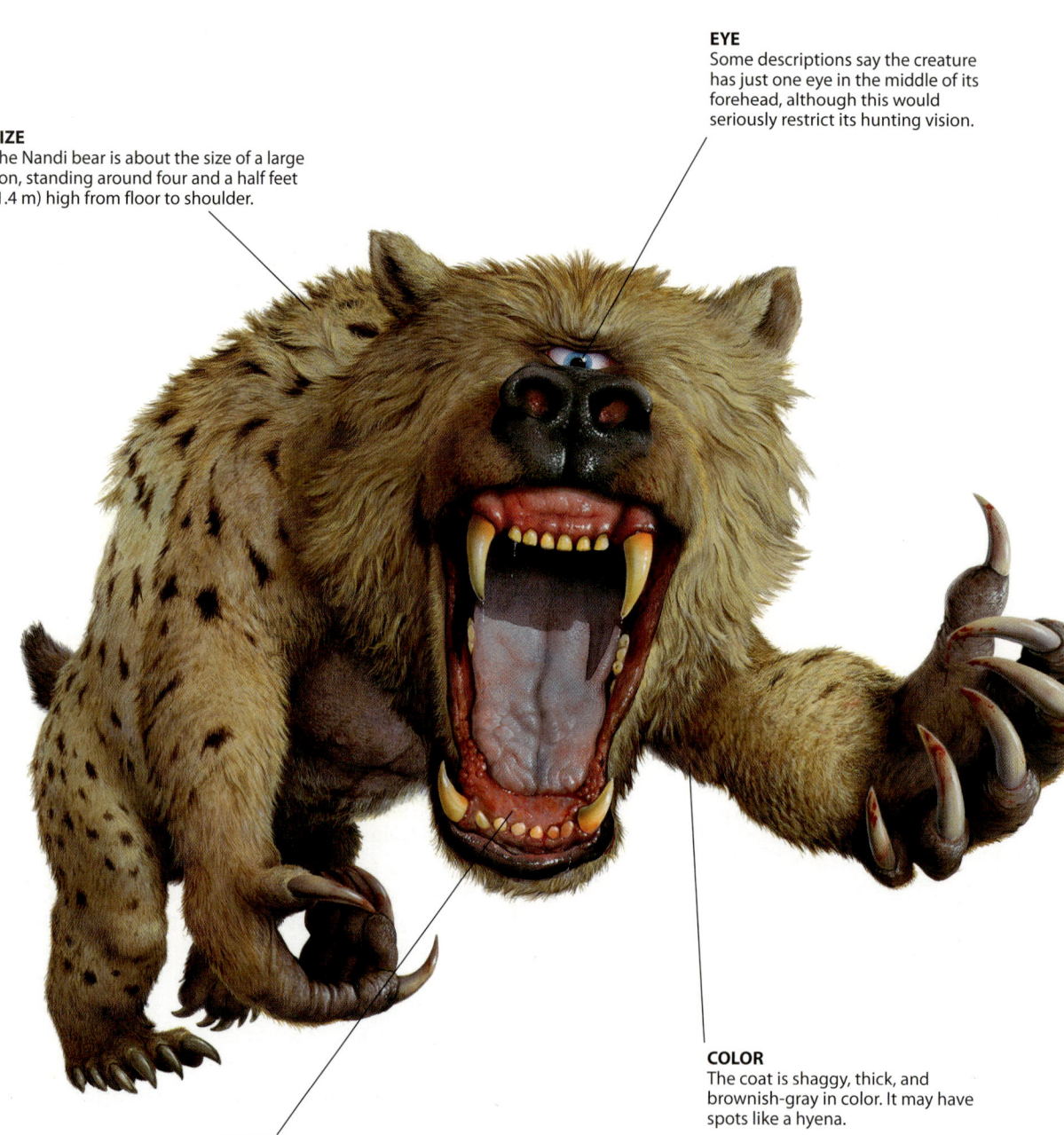

MOUTH
The bear's mouth is huge and gaping, and lined with enormous canines for tearing meat and massive back molars for crushing and grinding.

COLOR
The coat is shaggy, thick, and brownish-gray in color. It may have spots like a hyena.

NANDI BEAR

Described like a "dirty polar bear" the Nandi bear mystifies scientists. The reports are so convincing that people really think the creature exists, but surely it cannot be a bear, as there are no bears living in Africa! It walks like a bear but hunts like a hyena, attacking in the dark and tearing out the brains of its victims. People in the villages of this part of Kenya are fearful that it will raid their huts at night and steal their children. Shooting it seems to have no effect, but locals have tried to destroy the beast by burning a hut it has entered.

It is unusual, but not unheard of, for a hunter to travel alone when night is about to fall. Armed with a spear, this tribesman is taking the risk to get back to his family before dark. As he walks through the trees, he hears nothing except the usual sounds of the forest. Before he can defend himself, the Nandi bear makes its attack. A single swipe of its huge claws slashes off the top of the hunter's head. The bear can easily eat out his brain and leave the rest of his body for scavengers.

ACTUAL SIZE

WHERE IN THE WORLD?

The bear has been seen around western Kenya in Africa, and gets its name from the Kenyan Nandi tribe.

DID YOU KNOW?

• Local people have many names for the creature, including duba, kerit, chimosit, kikambangwe, vere, and sabrookoo.

• Bears have not lived in Africa since the atlas bear became extinct there in the 1800s. The descriptions match that of a hyena quite well, and some people have suggested that the monster is a giant, or even prehistoric, hyena.

• The Nandi bear can destroy whole herds of livestock. One farm reported nearly 70 sheep and goats had been destroyed, all by having their brains torn out. The bodies were otherwise untouched.

• In 1927, colonial Magistrate Captain Hichens set up camp to watch over a village that had been raided. His tent was destroyed and his dog was taken…but by what creature?

URBAN MYTHS AND LEGENDARY CREATURES

Ogopogo

HEAD
Many sightings agree that the monster has the head of a goat, although some describe it as more like a horse's head.

FINS
Descriptions of its back fin vary from one long rippling fin to several saw-toothed ridges on its back. Ogopogo has side fins to propel it through the water and a small tail to help steer its long, undulating body.

SIZE
Amateur videos taken of the monster show that it is at least 40 feet (12.2 m) long and maybe as much as 60 feet (18.3 m).

BODY
Some unexciting descriptions of Ogopogo say it looks like a log moving through the water. Others say that the body is humped.

OGOPOGO

The earliest descriptions of Ogopogo come from native Indians who lived by the lake. They call it N'Ha-a-itk, which means "Lake Demon." Legend says that the lake monster was originally a man who became possessed by a demon and murdered a local called Old Kan-He-Kan. This local man was highly respected, and in his memory the lake was called Okanagan. The Indian gods changed his murderer into a monster, doomed to dwell forever at the scene of his crime.

⚠ A farm worker by the name of John McDougall often had to cross Lake Okanagan. He was used to canoeing across with his team of horses swimming behind, and always made sure he dropped a peace offering such as a chicken in the center of the lake. On one sad occasion he forgot this offering, and was halfway across when he felt the rope around his horses being dragged suddenly downward. He could not save his team and had to cut the rope to save himself.

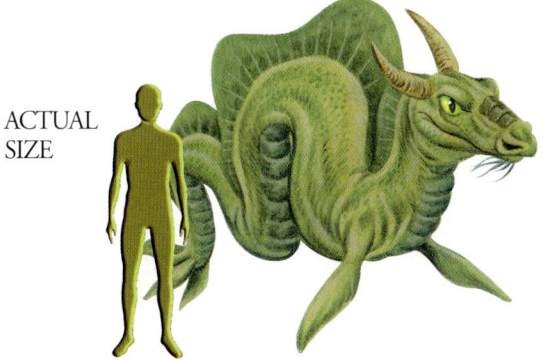

ACTUAL SIZE

WHERE IN THE WORLD?

BRITISH COLUMBIA

Lake Okanagan is a large, deep lake in the westernmost province of Canada, British Columbia.

DID YOU KNOW?

• The legend of Ogopogo is similar to that of the Loch Ness Monster but is even older. The monster is now the mascot of the city of Kelowna on the shores of the lake.

• The creature gained its name in 1912, when it was written about in a poem: "His mother was an earwig, his father was a whale, a little bit of head and hardly any tail—and Ogopogo was his name."

• In 2000, an expedition set out to prove the existence of Ogopogo, and took sonar recordings of a 50-foot (15.2-m) body in the depths of the lake, moving speedily.

• A 2008 expedition to track down the monster was filmed for a TV documentary and used thermal imaging, dive teams, sonar, and hydrosound technology.

URBAN MYTHS AND LEGENDARY CREATURES

Reptoid Alien

EYES
Huge and catlike, these are probably sensitive to infrared light, enabling a Reptoid to detect its prey in the dark, by body heat.

MUSCLES
Despite spending long periods in space, a Reptoid is always powerfully muscled.

SKIN
Tough and scaly, this is adapted to withstand injury from the prolonged bouts of physical violence the Reptoids indulge in. Some witnesses also say that it glows with a lime-green aura.

HANDS
These have just three fingers and an opposable thumb for gripping.

TONGUE
Just like reptiles, these aliens taste the air with a long, flicking forked tongue.

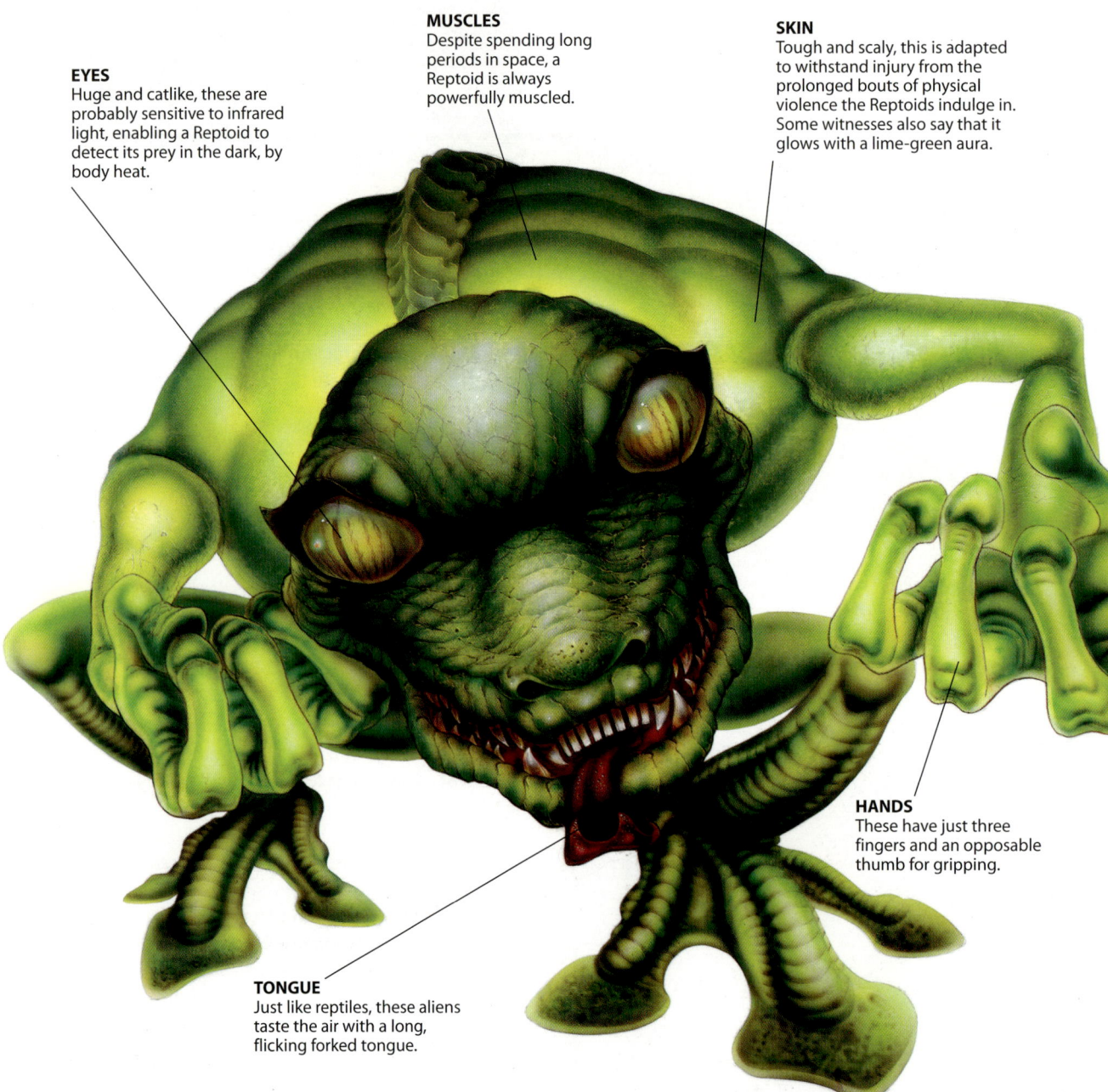

REPTOID ALIEN

These scaly monsters seem to enjoy kidnapping both animals and human beings—so keep an eye on the skies. Some people claim they are aliens, while others think they are descendants of the dinosaurs. Whatever the case, they have supposedly left a trail of horribly mutilated animals across the United States. As well as being brutal and violent, the Reptoid alien is also highly intelligent. It is feared by some that one day they may take control of our planet, putting humans into the chains of slavery.

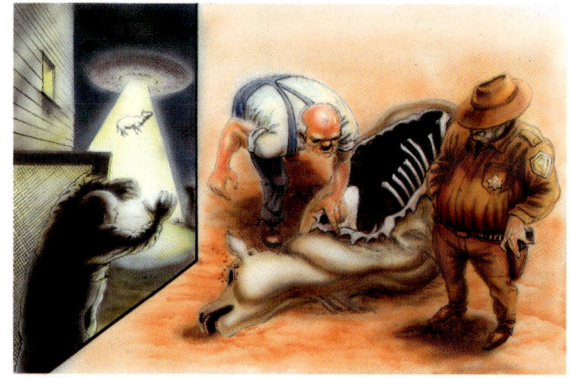

⚠ Stepping outside to investigate a strange noise, a farmer is alarmed to see a spaceship hovering overhead. He becomes even more agitated when one of his cows floats up into the alien craft. Next day, he finds one of his cows drained of blood and with its eyes, tongue, and innards surgically removed. But despite the evidence, the sheriff refuses to believe his story.

ACTUAL SIZE

WHERE IN THE WORLD?

Reports of Reptoid aliens come from around the world, but these entities are most active in remote areas of the United States.

DID YOU KNOW?

• Some experts speculate that the Reptoids consider a cow's blood and organs a delicacy. Others think they use the cows as an organic resource.

• Abductees say that the Reptoids come from the Draco star system.

• Some UFOlogists claim that the Reptoids avoid arousing suspicion by transporting their invasion force safely between stars in a massive spaceship disguised as a planet.

URBAN MYTHS AND LEGENDARY CREATURES

Skunk Ape

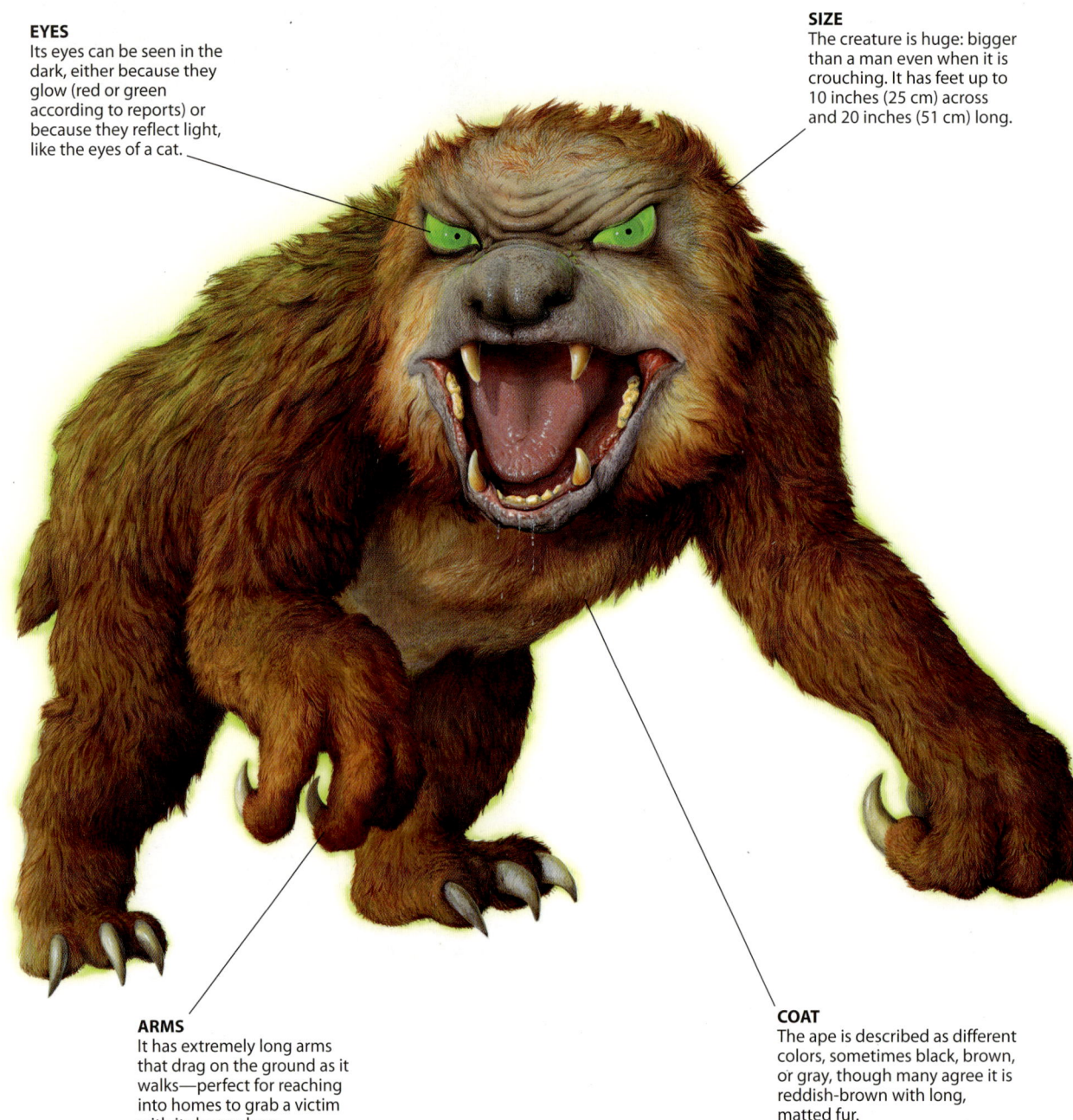

EYES
Its eyes can be seen in the dark, either because they glow (red or green according to reports) or because they reflect light, like the eyes of a cat.

SIZE
The creature is huge: bigger than a man even when it is crouching. It has feet up to 10 inches (25 cm) across and 20 inches (51 cm) long.

ARMS
It has extremely long arms that drag on the ground as it walks—perfect for reaching into homes to grab a victim with its huge claws.

COAT
The ape is described as different colors, sometimes black, brown, or gray, though many agree it is reddish-brown with long, matted fur.

SKUNK APE

Many parts of the world have their stories of giant, hairy creatures with massive limbs, huge feet, and big claws and teeth. Florida certainly has such a creature. It fits that description and then some, with a stink that warns people of its presence before it can even be seen or heard. The smell gives it its name, as it has the dreadful odor of a skunk—also described as old cabbage, animal dung, or rotting flesh. It may be a form of defense—it could roll in the bodies of its decaying victims to keep away attackers with the smell. It has a huge appetite for flesh and seems to prefer humans to any other animal. This creature is not frightened of humans either. It may hide in the undergrowth of swamplands, but when it has an appetite, it is not afraid to approach human homes for its feeding frenzy.

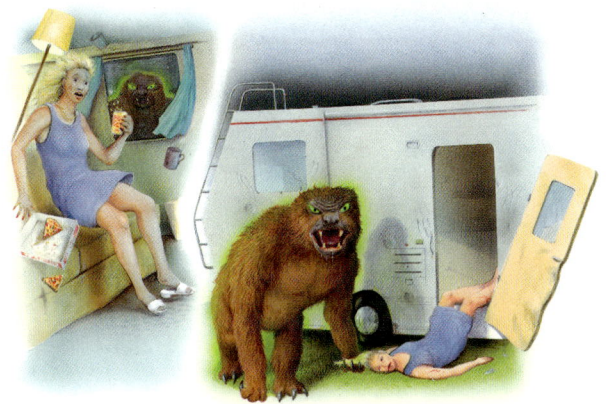

 The trailer parks of Florida are prime targets. The skunk ape can approach without worrying about yards and fences, and step right up to the door and wrench it off its hinges. The only clue the poor victim gets is a stench that is nauseating…they are about to become supper themselves.

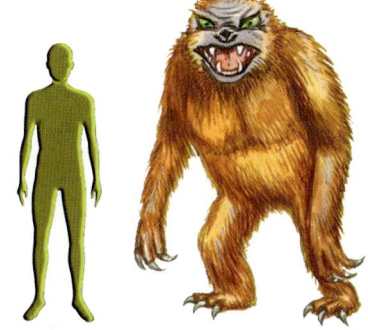

ACTUAL SIZE

WHERE IN THE WORLD?

The skunk ape has been sighted in Georgia, Arkansas, and North Carolina, but the majority of reports come from Florida, especially the Everglades.

DID YOU KNOW?

• One of the most recent sightings of the skunk ape was in Sarasota County. A woman took photos of a hairy creature, 7 feet (2 m) tall, that had been raiding fruit in her backyard. The photos are known as the Myakka photos.

• Even today, people undertake skunk ape expeditions to try and identify it. No one has any real evidence of footprints, fur, or a body.

• One tracker claimed to find sets of footprints of different sizes that suggest there are families of skunk apes lurking in the swamps.

• The stories of the skunk ape have been around for two centuries, told by Native Americans and frontiersmen alike.

URBAN MYTHS AND LEGENDARY CREATURES

Spring Heeled Jack

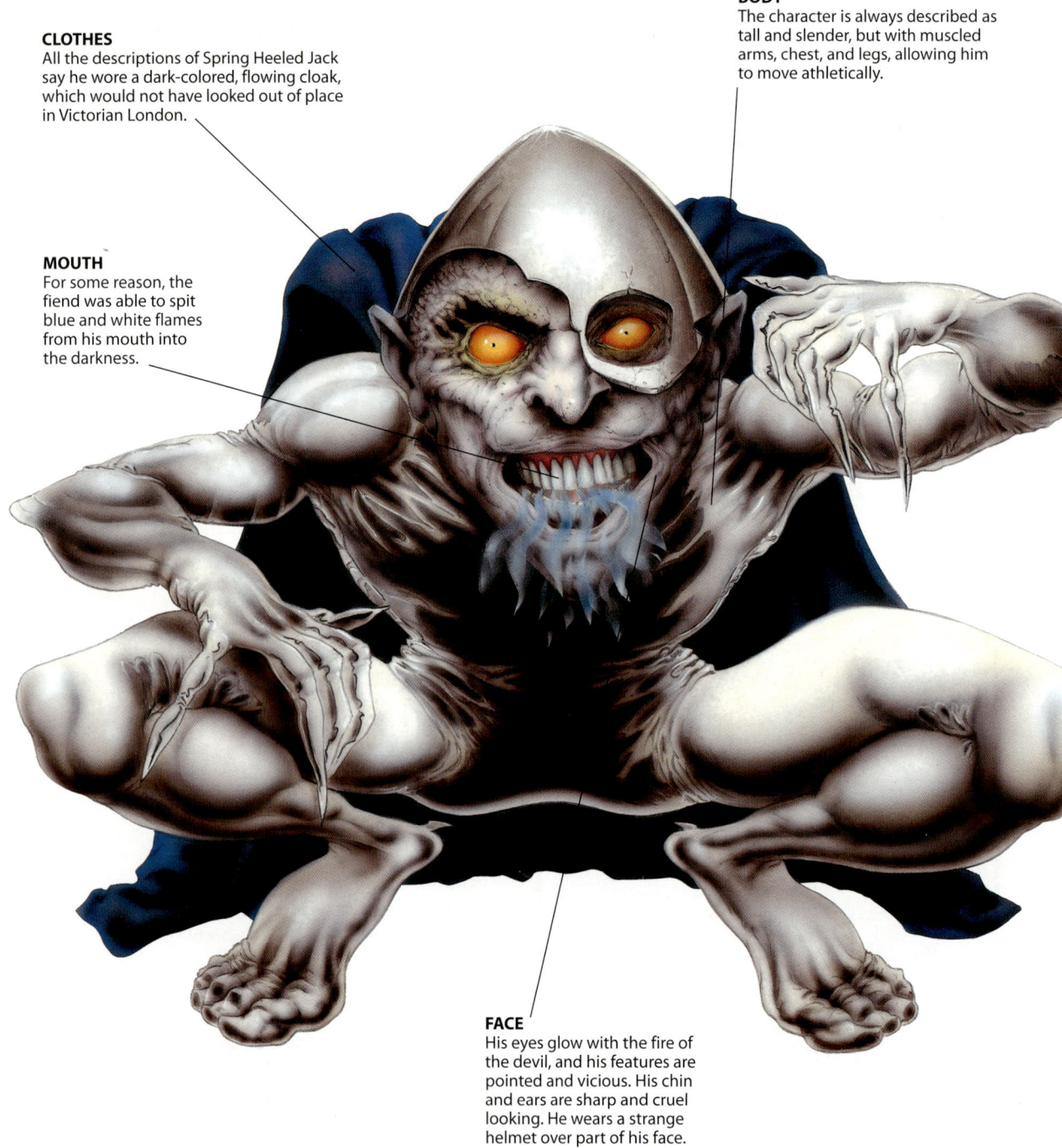

CLOTHES
All the descriptions of Spring Heeled Jack say he wore a dark-colored, flowing cloak, which would not have looked out of place in Victorian London.

MOUTH
For some reason, the fiend was able to spit blue and white flames from his mouth into the darkness.

BODY
The character is always described as tall and slender, but with muscled arms, chest, and legs, allowing him to move athletically.

FACE
His eyes glow with the fire of the devil, and his features are pointed and vicious. His chin and ears are sharp and cruel looking. He wears a strange helmet over part of his face.

SPRING HEELED JACK

Is this a character from fiction, a myth, or a real person? Who can know for sure? Spring Heeled Jack was first reported to the police in London in 1837, and it's thought he was last seen in Liverpool in 1904. He was certainly distinctive, not only for his appearance, but for his amazing athletic powers. He was said to be able to leap over a 10-foot (3-m) high fence and in one story even jumped right over a house. He usually spat flames in the face of the people he terrorized and often left such bad scratches on them that it was believed he had claws of metal.

 Many of Jack's victims were young women. Generally, he followed them toward their home, or jumped on them in an alley. He tore at their clothes, clawed at their body, often breathed fire, and laughed a wicked, demonic laugh before running away and jumping many feet to safety. As time went on, he seemed to grow braver, knocking on doors and scaring the servants who answered. Each time the police were called, they could do nothing to catch him. In 1838, he was declared "a public menace."

ACTUAL SIZE

WHERE IN THE WORLD?

LONDON

Spring Heeled Jack was infamous in the 19th century in the streets of old London, and his fame spread around the UK.

DID YOU KNOW?

• Twentieth-century versions of Spring Heeled Jack have been reported in Prague (Czech Republic) and Houston, Texas.

• Groups of "vigilantes" were formed to try to catch this man-monster. One of them included the great military commander, the Duke of Wellington.

• One possible explanation for the mystery is that Spring Heeled Jack was a wicked prankster with a taste for evil practical jokes. As time went on and his reputation grew, others may have disguised themselves and carried out similar crimes.

• Spring Heeled Jack became famous in a time when people loved to read—and believe—"Penny Dreadfuls." These were like early comics featuring fantastic characters that appealed to the public. Spring Heeled Jack was featured and became a big hit.

URBAN MYTHS AND LEGENDARY CREATURES

Thetis Lake Monster

FINS
The spikes around the lake monster's face may look like the fins of other aquatic creatures, but they are razor sharp and used for slashing at people.

SCALES
The monster is covered from head to toe with shiny scales like the scales of a fish.

HANDS
This creature's hands are webbed to help propel it through the water, with five long claws like daggers.

GILLS
As it can breathe both above and below water, it is likely that the monster has gills like a fish and lungs like a person.

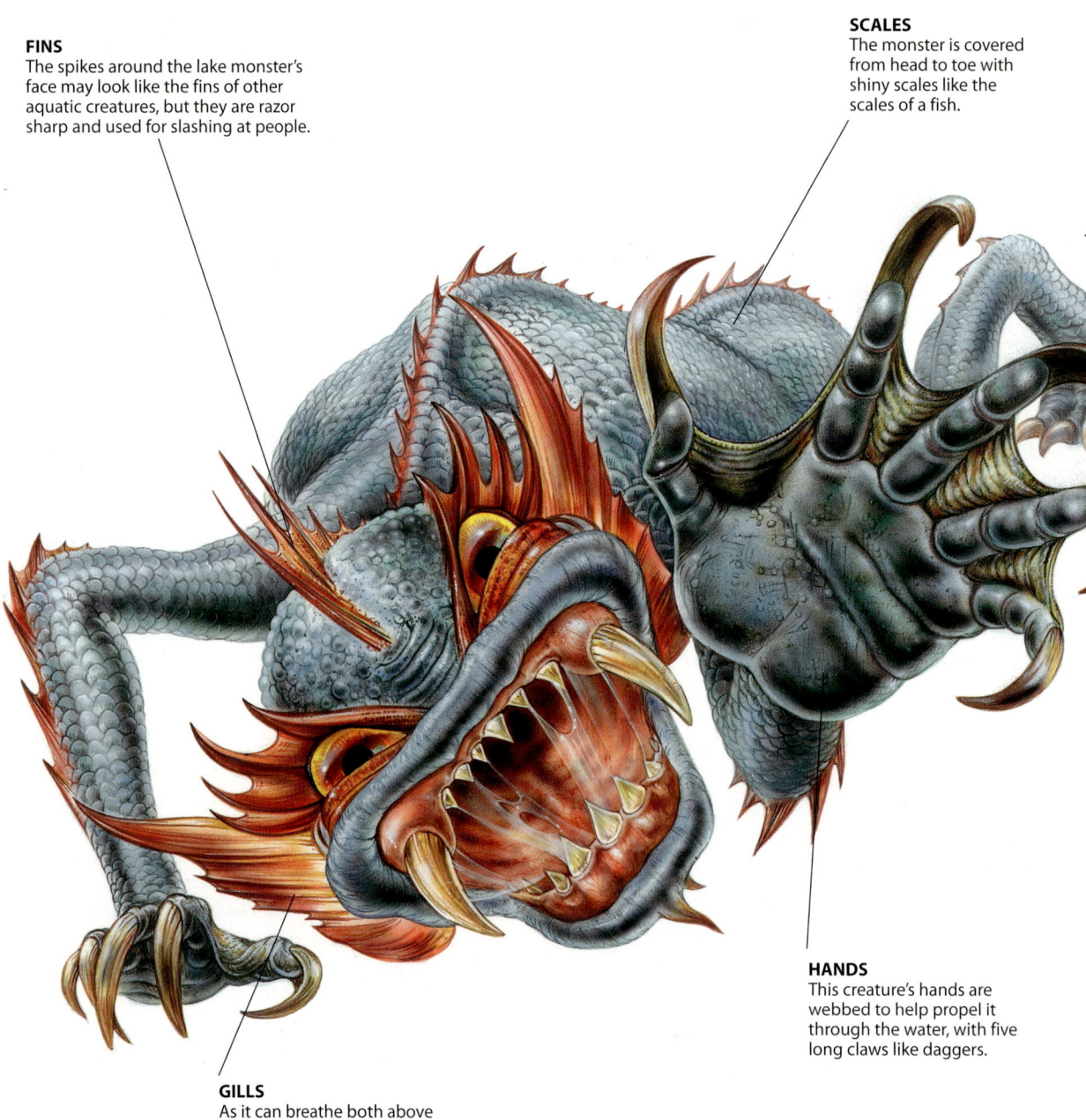

THETIS LAKE MONSTER

This monstrous creature has only been seen by a handful of people, and only in 1972. It reared up from the waters of Thetis Lake in Victoria, the capital of British Columbia, and chased people on the shores. It can stand to a height of around 5 feet (1.5 m) tall and run reasonably quickly up the beach. Its scaly body shimmers in the light, and it makes frightening, gurgling noises when it breathes out of water. Its eyes bulge from its head and it has huge ears—presumably adaptations to life in the dark, murky depths of the lake.

⚠ The first encounter with the monster of the lake was on August 19, 1972. Two boys saw the monster emerge from the water. Frightened, they began to move away, and the creature chased them, slashing out with its razor-sharp spikes. The terrified boys ran to the police and showed them the cuts one of them had been given. A few days later, the monster appeared on the opposite shore. This time, it emerged, looked around, and was seen by two others, but it did not attack. It hasn't been seen since.

ACTUAL SIZE

WHERE IN THE WORLD?

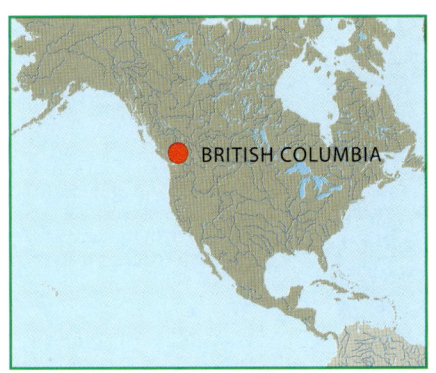

Inhabitants of British Columbia in Canada have more than their share of monsters.

DID YOU KNOW?

• The Royal Canadian Mounted Police started to search the lake for evidence of a creature living there. No reported evidence was found—no footprints, scales, or obvious signs of a place where the creature might live.

• The creature matches many descriptions of North American water monsters, and looks similar to the star of the 1954 movie, *The Creature from the Black Lagoon*.

• The police were later informed of a pet Tegu lizard that had gone missing, and concluded this may have been what was seen by the lake. Tegus grow to 3 or 4 feet (.9 to 1.2 m) long and walk on all fours, but they are vicious and scratch and bite when handled.

• The two teenagers who reported the first sighting have since admitted that they made the story up.

URBAN MYTHS AND LEGENDARY CREATURES

Tokoloshe

EYES
The eyes of a tokoloshe have been gouged out, but it uses its other senses to find its way around.

SKULL HOLE
The skull of a tokoloshe has a big hole made by a red-hot metal rod, such as a poker. The special power of heat plays a vital part in Zulu magic.

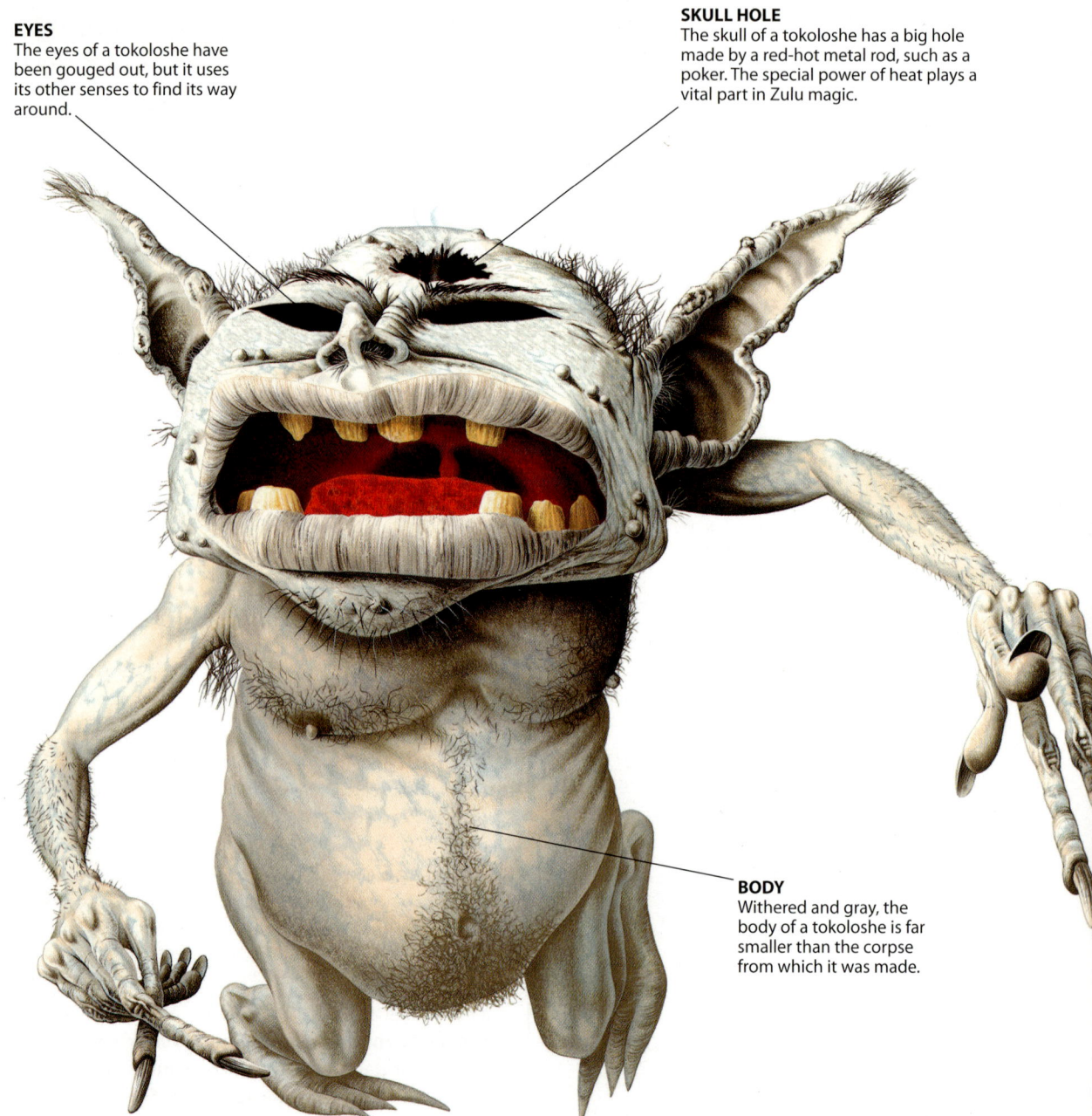

BODY
Withered and gray, the body of a tokoloshe is far smaller than the corpse from which it was made.

TOKOLOSHE

The tokoloshe is a twisted little creature. It lives in South Africa and is a cross between a zombie, a poltergeist, and a gremlin. Tokoloshes are created from dead bodies by shamen, or witch doctors, usually if the shaman has been offended by someone. Even though the tokoloshes are only the size of small children (the corpses shrivel up during the transformation), they can create terrible destruction. They attack people and property, often as the result of a curse. Worse still, only the person who is cursed will be able to see the tokoloshe—it is invisible to everyone else around. Once a tokoloshe is created, it will wander around causing mischief and mayhem.

 A woman has had an argument with a tribal elder and will pay the price. She arrives home to find a tokoloshe waiting. The diminutive creature leaps on the terrified victim, beating her with supernatural strength. The victim knows her bed is a haven from the horror. The bedstead is propped up on bricks that are wrapped in old paper, an ancient ploy against the fiend. The woman leaps onto the bed, safe from attack but powerless to protect her home. The tokoloshe rampages through her home, smashing her possessions with demonic delight.

WHERE IN THE WORLD?

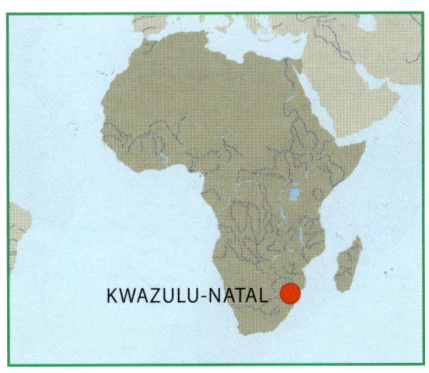

Tokoloshes have been reported throughout southern Africa, but they are most active in the South African province of KwaZulu-Natal. However, no area is safe from the fiends. Once a tokoloshe has been created, no one can know for sure where it may turn up.

ACTUAL SIZE

DID YOU KNOW?

• Tokoloshes have a strong dislike of schoolchildren and will often scribble on their schoolbooks or destroy their homework to get them into trouble with their teachers.

• Zulus usually blame misfortune on witchcraft. Suspected witches and their families are put to death and their property then given to the tribal chief.

• For some reason, wealthy villagers are far more likely to be accused of magic than poor people.

URBAN MYTHS AND LEGENDARY CREATURES

Yara-ma-yha-who

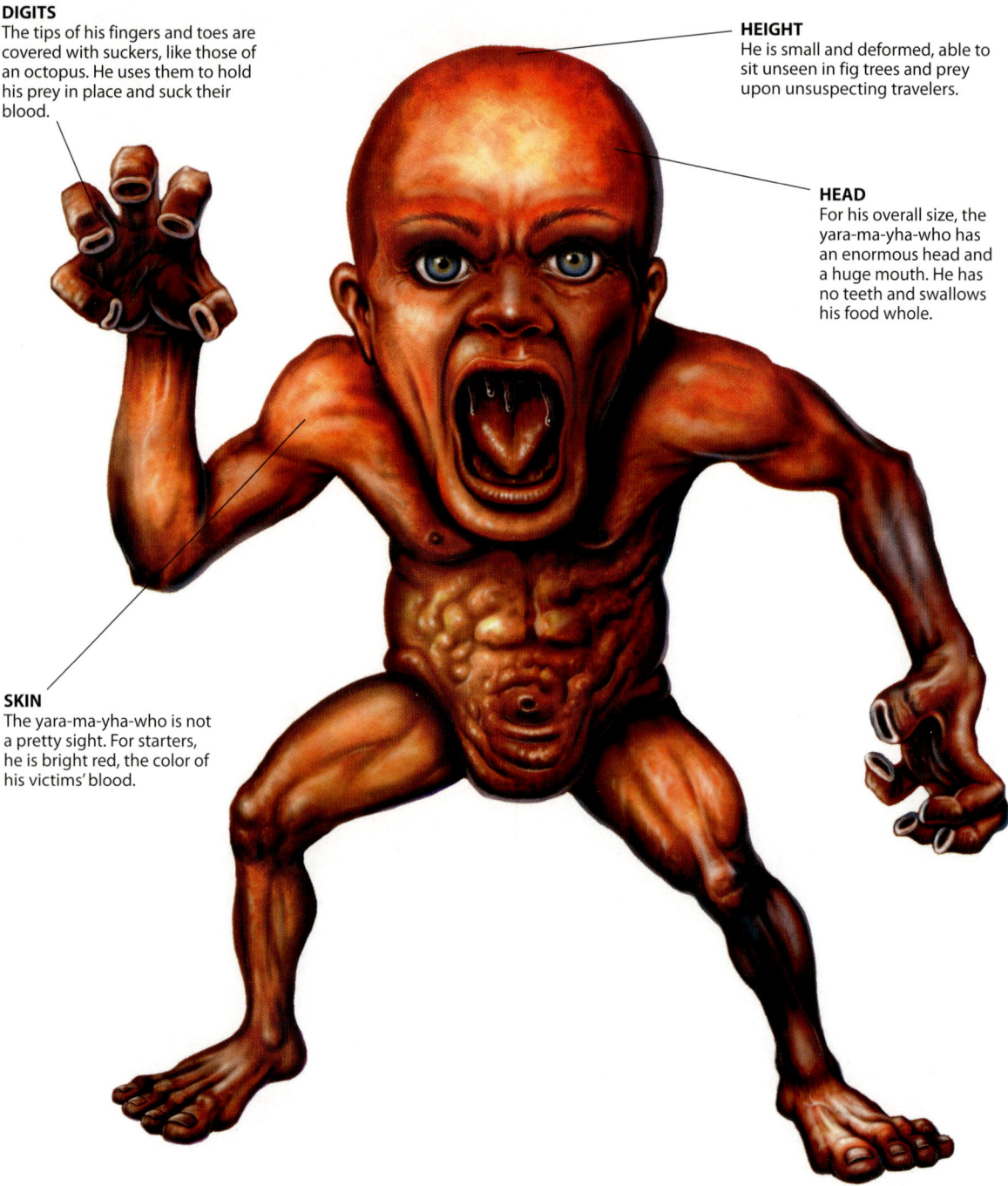

DIGITS
The tips of his fingers and toes are covered with suckers, like those of an octopus. He uses them to hold his prey in place and suck their blood.

HEIGHT
He is small and deformed, able to sit unseen in fig trees and prey upon unsuspecting travelers.

HEAD
For his overall size, the yara-ma-yha-who has an enormous head and a huge mouth. He has no teeth and swallows his food whole.

SKIN
The yara-ma-yha-who is not a pretty sight. For starters, he is bright red, the color of his victims' blood.

YARA-MA-YHA-WHO

How do you eat people if you have no teeth? If you're the yara-ma-yha-who from Australian aboriginal mythology, you swallow them whole! This evil creature lives in fig trees, where he waits for passersby to rest in the shade. He jumps on them, pins them down, and sucks out their blood. The weakened victim is alive, and the yara-ma-yha-who goes wandering to work up a real appetite. Upon his return, he gulps the victim like a snake swallowing its prey. Then, the creature stands up and dances to shake its food down to its stomach.

 Being eaten by the yara-ma-yha-who doesn't result in death. Instead, his victims are regurgitated after the yara-ma-yha-who has quenched his thirst with water and slept off his food coma. The victim is reborn, but is slightly shorter than before they were consumed. Several people have been caught more than once, getting shorter and redder each time they are brought back up. Eventually, the process is just too much, and the victim emerges as a wizened, red-skinned, vampiric creature—another yara-ma-yha-who has been created.

ACTUAL SIZE

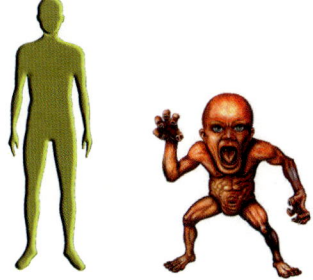

WHERE IN THE WORLD?

This wicked little vampire occupies many territories across Australia.

DID YOU KNOW?

• Usually, a victim can survive three attacks before he is turned into a yara-ma-yha-who himself.

• The best way to elude this vampire is to play dead. When he returns from his walk, pretend to be a corpse. He will tickle you and poke you with a stick to test whether you are truly lifeless.

• If you pass the tickle test, the yara-ma-yha-who will sit and watch from a distance, looking for any signs of life. He may fall asleep, giving you the chance to escape.

• Those who are lucky enough to reach this stage stand a strong chance of survival. The vampire's strange legs are not built for sprinting. In fact, he runs like a wobbling bird.

URBAN MYTHS AND LEGENDARY CREATURES

Yeti

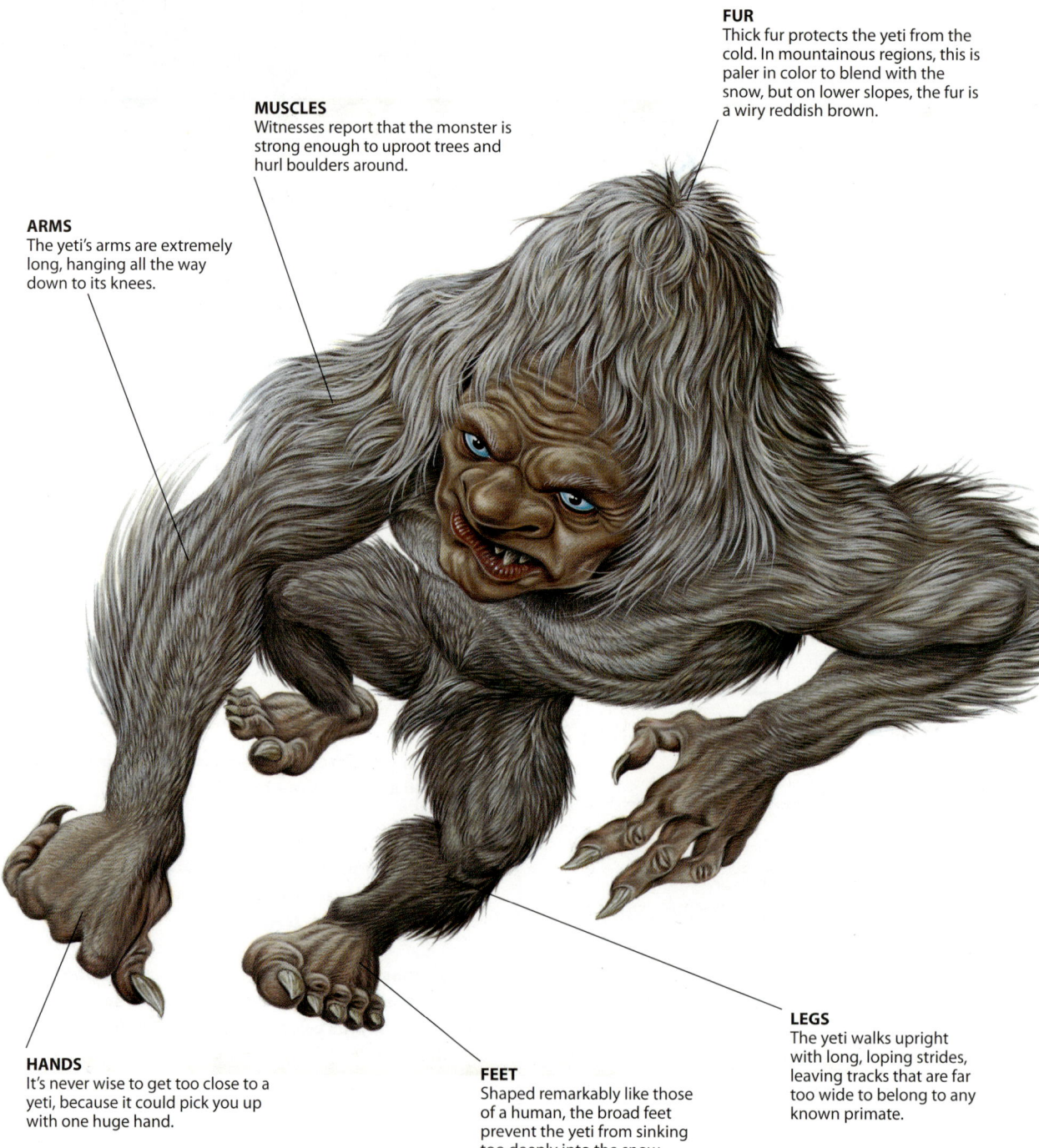

FUR
Thick fur protects the yeti from the cold. In mountainous regions, this is paler in color to blend with the snow, but on lower slopes, the fur is a wiry reddish brown.

MUSCLES
Witnesses report that the monster is strong enough to uproot trees and hurl boulders around.

ARMS
The yeti's arms are extremely long, hanging all the way down to its knees.

HANDS
It's never wise to get too close to a yeti, because it could pick you up with one huge hand.

FEET
Shaped remarkably like those of a human, the broad feet prevent the yeti from sinking too deeply into the snow.

LEGS
The yeti walks upright with long, loping strides, leaving tracks that are far too wide to belong to any known primate.

YETI

Tantalizing trails of oversized footprints are often the only indication of this hairy creature's presence as it wanders across the isolated slopes of the Himalayas. Both native Sherpas and foreign explorers have glimpsed this huge, upright figure loping across the snow. Yetis are territorial creatures, and are said to kill and eat those who wander into their territories. Local traditions describe three different types of yeti, the largest growing up to 15 feet (4.5 m) tall.

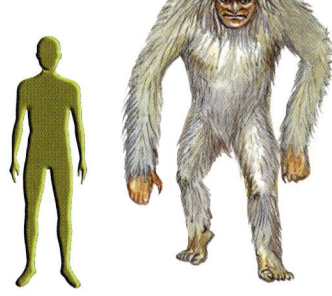

ACTUAL SIZE

▲ Lost in the heights of the Himalayan mountains, a lone mountaineer tries desperately to find his way back to civilization. But as he wanders blindly through the snow, he stumbles into the path of a huge yeti. Howling with rage, the hairy beast rushes over and grabs the climber by the arm, incensed that a stranger has blundered into its territory. Then, striding onto a ledge, the monster dangles the unfortunate victim over a cliff with one strong arm, before dropping the climber to his death on the rocks far below.

DID YOU KNOW?

• In 1961, the Nepalese government officially declared that yetis existed. It subsequently granted $10,000 licenses to any hunters dedicated and rich enough to stalk the beast through its Himalayan home.

• According to Sherpas, the yeti is partial to a drop or two of alcohol.

• The best way to escape from a yeti is by running downhill. Any yeti attempting to follow will be blinded by the immense tangle of hair falling into its face and covering its eyes.

• Some people think the yeti has transparent second eyelids, which protect its eyes during blizzards.

• The name "yeti" is a Tibetan word meaning "magical creature," but the Nepalese also know the beast as "rakshas," the demon. The Chinese call it the "alma," while another Tibetan word for the beast, "metoh-kangmi," is often translated as the "abominable snowman."

WHERE IN THE WORLD?

The yeti is found in the Himalayan mountain range in Asia, with most sightings occurring in Nepal, Bhutan, and Tibet. But some enthusiasts have also linked the yeti with reports of similar-looking creatures such as the North American monster, Bigfoot.

GUIDE TO URBAN MYTHS AND LEGENDARY CREATURES

The Beast of Bray Road
Area: Wisconsin
Features: Large, heavy body; powerful chest; covered in gray-brown hair; eyes glow yellow; snout; pointed ears; fangs

Bigfoot
Area: North America
Features: More than 3 feet 3 inches (1 m) wide and 6 feet 6 inches (2 m) tall; looks like an ape; green or yellow eyes; shaggy coat; long arms hang down to its knees

Bunyip
Area: Australia, Tasmania
Features: Dark and hairy; giant clawed hands; sometimes described as dog-like, sometimes horse-like; eyes burn like fire

Goatman
Area: Maryland
Features: Part man, part goat; strong legs with hooves; horns; covered in tufts of black hair

Hopkinsville Goblin
Area: Kentucky
Features: Body too small for its head; smooth skin shimmers; long, slender arms; bony fingers with curving talons; bulging eyes; slit-like mouth; big, bat-like ears

Jersey Devil
Area: New Jersey
Features: Body of a dog or horse; short forelegs; walks upright on hind legs; bat-like wings; horns; head like a donkey with a dog's nose and teeth; rotten gums

Kongamoto
Area: Zambia, Zimbabwe
Features: A flying reptile; leathery wings; bird-like head; beak has sharp teeth; strong legs with powerful talons

Loch Ness Monster
Area: Loch Ness
Features: Long neck; flippers; stubby tail; forward-pointing eyes; needle-sharp teeth; humpbacked

Mngwa
Area: Kenya, Tanzania
Features: Cat as big as a donkey; gray fur; padded paws with claws; short jaws

Mokele-Mbembe
Area: Gabon, Cameroon, Congo
Features: As large as an elephant or hippo; long, muscular tail; head has horns or spikes on top; long neck

Morgawr
Area: Cornwall
Features: Long neck; humps on its back; rows of sharp teeth; could be longer than 20 feet (6.1 m)

Nandi Bear
Area: Kenya
Features: Size of a large lion; might have just one eye in the middle of its forehead; huge mouth with massive teeth; shaggy, thick, brownish-gray coat

Ogopogo
Area: British Columbia
Features: Back and side fins; goat-like or horse-like head; might be as long as 60 feet (18.3 m); may have a humped body or look like a log in the water

Reptoid Alien
Area: United States
Features: Tough, scaly skin; glows lime green; long, forked tongue; huge, catlike eyes; muscular; three fingers and thumb on its hands

Skunk Ape
Area: Florida
Features: Bigger than a man; reddish-brown, long, matted fur; long arms that drag on the ground; eyes glow red or yellow; smells bad

Spring Heeled Jack
Area: London
Features: Tall and slender; muscular arms and legs; wears a dark-colored cloak; mouth spits flames; eyes glow with fire; wears a helmet over part of his face

Thetis Lake Monster
Area: British Columbia
Features: Razor-sharp fins; shiny scales; can breathe above and below water; webbed hands; dagger-like claws

Tokoloshe
Area: KwaZulu-Natal
Features: Size of a child; shriveled corpse; eyes have been gouged out; hole made by a hot poker in its head

Yara-ma-yha-who
Area: Australia
Features: Small and deformed; bright-red skin; fingers and toes have suckers on them; big head and mouth

Yeti
Area: Himalayas
Features: Thick white or reddish-brown fur; broad, human-like feet; huge hands; long arms dangling to the ground; strong muscles

Glossary

agitate: excite

amateur: someone who likes to do something and does not get paid for it

flexible: bendable

incense: to anger

invulnerable: not able to be hurt

isolate: to keep away from other people

luminous: shining

malevolent: doing mean things for enjoyment

mutation: a change in form

partial: to like

protruding: sticking out

pummel: to hit many times

rampage: out-of-control actions

ravenous: very hungry

regurgitate: to throw up

remnant: just a piece left

soot: ashes

sophisticated: grown up

tempt: to promise someone gains for doing a task

transparent: see-through

undulating: wavy movement

unscathed: not harmed

wield: to use well

For More Information

Books

Emmer, Rick. *Loch Ness Monster: Fact or Fiction?* New York, NY: Chelsea House, 2010.

Incredible Popular Misconceptions. Edison, NJ: Chartwell Books, 2006.

Redmond, Shirley-Raye. *The Jersey Devil.* Farmington Hills, MI: KidHaven Press, 2009.

Townsend, John. *Mysterious Urban Myths.* Chicago, IL: Raintree, 2004.

Walker, Kathryn, and Brian Innes. *Mysteries of Giant Humanlike Creatures.* New York, NY: Crabtree Publishing Company, 2009.

Web Sites

Bigfoot Photo and Video Gallery
www.oregonbigfoot.com/gallery.php
See pictures and information about Bigfoot sightings.

Bunyips
www.nla.gov.au/exhibitions/bunyips/
Learn more about Bunyips and other Aboriginal tales.

Legend of Nessie
www.nessie.co.uk/index.html
Find out the latest Nessie sightings and information.

Publisher's note to educators and parents: Our editors have carefully reviewed these Web sites to ensure that they are suitable for students. Many Web sites change frequently, however, and we cannot guarantee that a site's future contents will continue to meet our high standards of quality and educational value. Be advised that students should be closely supervised whenever they access the Internet.

Index

abominable snowman 7, 43
Africa 17, 21, 23, 27, 39
alma 7, 43
Asia 43
Australia 9, 41, 44, 45
Beast of Bray Road 4, 5, 44
Bhutan 43
Bigfoot 5, 6, 7, 43, 44
British Columbia 7, 29, 37, 45
Bunyip 8, 9, 44
Cameroon 17, 23, 44
Canada 7, 29, 37
Cherokee 13
Congo 23, 44
Cornwall 25, 45
Creature from the Black Lagoon, The 37
cryptozoologists 5
England 25
Florida 33, 45
Gabon 23, 44
Gigantopithecus 7
Goatman 10, 11, 44
gremlin 39
Hopkinsville Goblin 12, 13, 44
hyena 26, 27
Himalayas 43, 45
Indians 29
Jersey Devil 14, 15, 44
Kentucky 13, 44
Kenya 21, 27, 44, 45
Kongamoto 16, 17, 44
KwaZulu-Natal 39, 45
"Lake Demon" 29
"living dinosaur" 22, 23
Loch Ness 19, 44
Loch Ness Monster 18, 19, 23, 25, 29, 44
London 34, 35, 45
"magical creature" 43
Maryland 11, 44
metoh-kangmi 43
mngwa 20, 21, 44
mokele-mbembe 22, 23, 44
morgawr 24, 25, 45
Myakka photos 33
Namibia 17
Nandi bear 21, 26, 27, 45
Native American 5, 33
Nepal 43
Nessie 18, 19
Nessitera rhombopteryx 19
New Jersey 15, 44
N'Ha-a-itk 29
North America 7, 37, 43, 44
nunda 21
Ogopogo 28, 29, 45
Olitau 17
"one that stops the flow of rivers" 23
plesiosaurs 18, 24, 25
poltergeist 39
pterodactyl 17
pterosaur 17
rakshas 43
Reptoid alien 30, 31, 45
Scottish Highlands 19
"sea giant" 25
shaman 39
Sherpas 43
skunk ape 32, 33, 45
Spring Heeled Jack 34, 35, 45
"strange one" 21
Tanzania 21, 44
Tasmania 9, 44
"terror of the coastlands" 21
Thetis Lake Monster 36, 37, 45
Tibet 43
tokoloshe 38, 39, 45
United States 7, 11, 31, 33, 45
vampire 41
werewolf 5
Wisconsin 5, 44
yara-ma-yha-who 40, 41, 45
yeti 7, 42, 43, 45
Zambia 17, 44
Zeuglodon (Basilosaurus) 19
Zimbabwe 17, 44
zombie 39
Zulus 38, 39